111: A Call to the Life of the Kingdom

111: A Call to the Life of the Kingdom

Mark D. Hampton

FOREWORD BY
Will Willimon

RESOURCE *Publications* · Eugene, Oregon

111: A CALL TO THE LIFE OF THE KINGDOM

Resource Publications
An Imprint of Wipf and Stock Publishers
199 W. 8th Ave., Suite 3
Eugene, OR 97401

www.wipfandstock.com

PAPERBACK ISBN: 978-1-6667-4706-5
HARDCOVER ISBN: 978-1-6667-4707-2
EBOOK ISBN: 978-1-6667-4708-9

08/25/22

Dedicated to:
The students whom I have had
the blessing to serve over the years.

With special thanks to:
My wife, Laura, for her endless support,
belief, and encouragement in all things
&
Emily Williams, for her tremendous help
editing and revising this work.

In memory of:
Dr. James W. Bryant (1936-2014), who first challenged me and
so many others to memorize the Sermon on the Mount.

Foreword

ALTHOUGH I'VE SPENT A lifetime attempting to preach the gospel, it saddens me that most of my listeners still can't tell the difference between a thinking, caring, sensitive American and a Christian. They still confuse the Kingdom of God with the USA, Inc., reducing the shock of Jesus Christ to common sense that's already believed by nine-out-of-ten Americans.

Not my former star student, Mark Hampton. Mark believes that there's not much wrong with contemporary Christians or today's church that can't be cured by listening to Jesus preach. Having had the Sermon on the Mount change his life, Mark invites us to share his excitement about and gratitude for Jesus' most famous sermon. He hears Jesus' sermon as an invitation to take up citizenship in a new realm, the Kingdom of God, to carry two passports in our pockets, to wake up and realize that in the presence and preaching of crucified, resurrected Jesus Christ, a whole new world was made available to us.

You'll be changed as Mark guides you through each surprising, revealing turn in the Sermon. Much of Mark's life could be described as his attempt to recover from the initial shock of hearing, really hearing, the Sermon on the Mount while he was a student in college. Now, as a talented, bright young pastor and preacher himself, Mark knows how to enable Jesus' words to leap off the page and grab us too, shaking us up and down, and opening our ears and our hearts to a fresh adventure with ancient, beloved Scripture.

Mark makes these devotionals into a journey whereby we are taken, day-by-day, step-by-step closer toward more permanent residence in the Kingdom of God, that blessed realm where our values are turned upside down and we are surprised to find God as the one who wants both to bless us in our need and to call us into his service.

"And when Jesus finished these sayings, the crowds were astonished at his teaching . . . " (Matt 7:28). By the time you finish this book, you are sure to have heard a call to a life with Christ that will surprise you as well. Get ready to be astonished.

"Too many American Christians want to worship a King without taking up responsibility for life in the Kingdom," I heard a veteran church observer grouse the other day. We've attempted to refashion Jesus into a savior who's more comfortable and conducive to our cultural context, detached from the world he says he has come to save. Mark Hampton will have none of this. He believes that our salvation lies in the courage to attend carefully to Jesus' most memorable sermon, to accept the Sermon's call to life in the kingdom, depart on a journey toward God, and to adapt ourselves to the kingdom's demands rather than rework Jesus' reign to a regime more to our liking.

Welcome to a wonderful journey. You couldn't have a better guide than Mark Hampton.

Will Willimon, Professor of the Practice of Christian Ministry, Duke Divinity School, United Methodist bishop, retired, and author of Accidental Preacher: A Memoir.

Introduction

I REMEMBER SITTING IN shock during my very first class of Bible College. As my classmates and I sat there, we squirmed in our seats as we were told that we would be required to memorize the Sermon on the Mount in its entirety. Naturally, we turned to Matthew's Gospel to see how long the Sermon is. Three whole chapters! At first, I thought the task was impossible, but I gave myself wholeheartedly to it, determined to ace the assignment.

So began my journey with the Sermon. I recorded myself reading the Sermon, then I listened to it every day on my commute to school and then back home. A total of about 70 minutes each day, four days a week. That works out to listening to the Sermon about 20 times a week. Expanded over the semester, I listened to these three chapters from Matthew's Gospel over 300 times.

This, by far, has been one of the most spiritually enriching practices I have ever engaged in. Each day I found myself challenged in a new way. Verses that I moved through without a thought some days would come back full force the next. There were many days with tears, and I remember hearing portions of the Sermon and my gut reaction being, "Ouch, that hurts!" God's Word truly is a double-edged sword, cutting to the deepest parts of who we are, able to divide joint and marrow. Sometimes this hurt, as I realized that I had not sought the kingdom as I should. I found myself exposed before the Word of God at countless moments, struck by the words of Jesus that so poignantly addressed my sin.

At the end of that first semester of Bible college, I sat down to write out the Sermon for my final examination. The fruit of my labor had paid off, and I was able to complete the final assignment with ease. However, the journey to do so is one I will never forget. Never before had I encountered God's Word in such a powerful way. Each day, as I allowed the words of the Sermon to pour over me, I was continually formed, shaped, and refashioned by God's Word. I was also given a profoundly intimate knowledge of the text, knowing the intricacies and nuances of the text and how each part related to the whole. I was able to see things I would not have seen if I had just read through it once or twice.

This is one of the experiences that has left an indelible mark on my pursuit of Christ. In fact, nothing else has ever really come close. I completed countless other assignments in Bible College and seminary, but none has had such a profound effect as this nor gave birth to such a rich experience with God's Word. At countless moments, it was as if I were sitting right there with the Master himself, hearing the words as they were first spoken. My friend, my hope is that this devotion offers you a similar experience. I believe that if you embrace the Sermon with the same enthusiasm as I did so many years ago, it will have the same effect in your life, too.

About the Sermon

The Sermon on the Mount introduces a radically different way of being in the world. It introduces us to the Kingdom of Heaven that is crashing into our present world through the life of Christ. The beatitudes (Matt 5:3-12) provide us a picture of what this kingdom looks like, and the rest of the Sermon describe what it looks like to live out the beatitudes.

Due to the nature of the kingdom, the Sermon is both *here*, but *not yet* fully present. It is *here* in the sense that Christ has lived and perfected the Sermon and calls his disciples to do the same. But it is also *not yet* in that we cannot achieve this by our own ability and striving. However, through the work of the Holy Spirit, we are being sanctified so that we may live as true citizens of this kingdom. Jesus preached that the "kingdom is at hand," and in the Sermon he now calls for his disciples to live out the values of the Kingdom of Heaven.

This will be difficult work. When I read through the Sermon, I recognize that it claims my entire life, yet I so unwillingly yield my life to it. This devotional, then, is in many ways a story of my own failures. I have sought to embrace the teachings that Christ lays out here, but they are not easy in any regard. I feel as though I am pursuing an elusive Messiah who is impossible to catch. When I think that I have achieved some success in one area, the Sermon rips the mask off my face and exposes the countless other ways I am a hypocrite.

You might feel the same way at times as you dig deep into the Sermon. Don't be discouraged. That is God working! That is God revealing the areas of your life that need to be brought into conformity with Christ's teaching. When you feel discouraged or convicted, that is God working to grow you in those areas. Embrace those moments, knowing that the Holy Spirit will see you through and bring about fruit in your life.

How to Use this Devotional

This devotional has an odd length. Why 111 days? Typically, devotional books are based on the calendar, lasting 30, 60, or 90 days, and even up to a full year. This one does not follow a calendar, but it is intended to be used daily for 111 days. That is because it is based on the verses of Mathew chapters 5-7, rather than the calendar. Within those chapters is the Sermon on the Mount, which is comprised of 111 verses.

One verse is detailed in each day's devotion. However, none is separated from the verses surrounding it. That is because each verse *MUST* be read within its context, as with any passage of the Bible. Without doing so, the context is broken and the meaning is lost. This has been the perennial abuse of so many verses of the Sermon (e.g., "Judge not, that you be not judged." (Matt 7:1)). Though each devotion deals with an individual verse, it does so in consideration of the whole context of the Sermon. Each verse is so weighty and full of wisdom that it deserves its own attention, but attention has been given to it in light of the rest of the Sermon.

As you read through this Sermon, I encourage you not to ignore the context. To do so, I recommend having your Bible open to the Sermon each time you read this book. I also recommend beginning with the Sermon before you read anything in this book, as God's Word will speak with infinitely more power than anything written in these pages. Having done that, then move into the devotional for the day. I encourage you to read all the verses of the Sermon leading up to today's devotional. Thus, you would follow such a pattern:

Day 1—Read Matthew 5:1, then the devotional, then the questions

Day 2—Read Matthew 5:1-2, then the devotional, then the questions

Day 3—Read Matthew 5:1-5:3, then the devotional, then the questions

. . .

Day 111—Read Matthew 5:1-7:29, then the devotional,
then the questions

This may sound long and tedious, but it really is not. The Sermon on the Mount takes about 15 minutes or less to read on its own, and each devotional should not take longer than 5 minutes. So, on the very last day in which you read the entirety of the Sermon, it should only require about 20 minutes of reading. Furthermore, as you read through the Sermon, again and again, it will read more quickly each time.

As you do this, I also encourage you to memorize the verse for the day. By the end of 111 days, you will then have memorized the entire sermon. You will be well acquainted with God's Word and you will possess an intimacy with God's Word you cannot possibly imagine. When you do this, you are writing the kingdom on your heart. Then, once written on your heart, it will unfold in your life, blessing God, your neighbor, and yourself.

An Invitation

This devotional is an invitation to that same journey I embarked upon at the beginning of Bible College. You may not choose to memorize the Sermon, but I would encourage you to do so if possible. Writing God's Word on your heart will be a long, arduous, and even painful process. It will bring conviction at times, but that is the Holy Spirit working to sanctify you into the image of Christ. If you do this, the reward will be eternal. The Sermon will dwell richly in your heart and be a blessing to your days that follow, forever.

My friend, let us walk up the mountain and sit at the feet of the Master. His mouth is the fount of all wisdom, and all the treasures that are to be found in this world are in his words.

Day 1: Seeing the crowds, he went up on the mountain, and when he sat down, his disciples came to him. (Matt 5:1)

JESUS BEGINS HIS MOST iconic speech in a peculiar way, he retreats from the public. Rather than going to the streets or a crowded marketplace, he goes to a mountain. Remote, isolated, and not immediately accessible. He sees the crowds, but he then proceeds to go away from them. We might wonder why such a strange strategy. Why not go directly to the streets where the people are? In today's culture of mass media and ubiquitous advertising, Jesus' strategy appears inefficient and counterintuitive to the goal of teaching and preaching. Although it may seem odd to us, Jesus seems to be quite intentional about this method.

His goal is not to deliver a sermon for the masses but one that is, instead, for a targeted audience. It's for his disciples who come to him and sit at his feet to learn the ways of the Master. Jesus does not speak to those who are not his followers, but to his disciples. Alone. He is teaching them what the life of following him looks like. He does not tell them that if they obey these words they will truly be his followers. Instead, he is stating that since they are his followers their lives need to follow a particular pattern. Friends, today this is our call as well: to sit at the feet of the Master and see what he requires of our lives.

Jesus' words are radically different, they defy our own agendas and fly in the face of the status quo, all so that we may truly live the life that Christ calls us to. But, to do so, we must leave the places of familiarity in our lives and instead go to the mountain. It is there that we will truly find what it means to follow Christ. We do not go to the teachings of this world that incessantly confront us from every angle. No, we go to the words of a prophet, priest, and king which have persisted throughout the ages.

Have you left the comforts of this world to sit at Jesus' feet? What prevents you from coming to the mountain? What do you fear you will leave behind?

Day 2: And he opened his mouth and
taught them, saying . . . (5:2)

JESUS IS A TEACHER. We may easily rush past that simple little notion, yet it is actually quite profound when we stop to consider what it means to teach. Jesus is passing along knowledge that he possesses that his disciples do not have quite yet. He is handing on skills that he has mastered, leading the disciples graciously by the hand to demonstrate what this life of following him entails. He is forming them, shaping them to be a different type of people in this world, a people who are marked by radical obedience to a life that sacrificially gives itself up again and again.

Jesus purposefully acts as an instructor for the life of following him and living as he does. When we consider this, we see that those who are learning from this Master must change both their way of thinking and their behavior to truly learn the lesson. They cannot simply have the knowledge in their minds, but they must incorporate it into their lives. Obviously, this is not the simplest of lesson plans. To learn these lessons ourselves, we must massively realign priorities, abandon notions of self-reliance, and live to a radically higher standard than we would ever choose for ourselves.

Though this may seem too difficult, this is what the lesson plan requires. We'll see this as we move through the Sermon on the Mount. Whenever this call seems too high, or the lesson too difficult, we must also remember who we have for a teacher. We must remember that the Lord Jesus Christ is our teacher, and he is the most gracious of teachers. And not only gracious, for he is also our perfect example of what it means to live the Sermon on the Mount. Now, if the best teachers produce the best students, then we are in the best of hands. We are well positioned to be shaped the way Christ desires us to be, formed into the image of our great Teacher. Yet, to do so, we must do as the disciples did. We must go up the mountain and sit under the teaching of the Master.

*Have you taken on the posture of being a student of Jesus' words? Who
are the teachers in your life, and what lessons are they teaching you?*

Day 3: "Blessed are the poor in spirit, for theirs
is the kingdom of heaven." (5:3)

A PROFESSOR ONCE TOLD me, "Do you know why Jesus begins with the poor in spirit? Because by the end of the Sermon you're going to realize that's you!" As I've read through the Sermon time after time, I've found this to be true. I read the words of Jesus and it becomes glaringly apparent that, before God, I truly am poor in spirit. But, wouldn't we naturally think that it is those who are rich in spirit who are blessed? However, Jesus tells us that it is the other way around. It is those who are poor and lowly in spirit who are blessed and will inherit the Kingdom of Heaven.

So, what does it mean to be poor in spirit? It means having an honest appraisal of ourselves before God. It means recognizing that God is holy, and we are not. It's seeing that the gap between God and ourselves is a rather large one. If we think otherwise, the lessons of the Sermon will correct our thinking. We cannot read its words and see ourselves as having fulfilled Christ's commands. If we think we have, we only deceive ourselves. So, how are we to inherit this kingdom that Jesus is teaching about? If the gap between ourselves and God is so large, how can we even begin to bridge that gap and live as true citizens of the Kingdom of Heaven?

Friend, let me remind you of what a magnificent teacher we truly have. We have a teacher who bridges the gap on our behalf. Jesus is the perfect example of the Sermon, and through his life, death, and resurrection, he has already begun to usher in the Kingdom of Heaven. It is *here*, but *not yet* fully present. The eternal is crashing into the everyday through Christ's work, and the Holy Spirit is working in you and me to form and shape us into the image of our Messiah. Because of this, we can seek the Kingdom of Heaven in our lives now. To do so, the first step is to recognize how truly poor in spirit we are before God.

Have you ever made an honest appraisal of yourself, or do you consider yourself righteous? How does an honest assessment of ourselves before God enable us to pursue God's holiness?

Day 4: "Blessed are those who mourn, for they shall be comforted." (5:4)

IF THE FIRST BEATITUDE doesn't seem too absurd, certainly the second one does. How can we read this and not think it foolish? Those who mourn are blessed? Another way to translate the phrase could be, "exceedingly happy are those who mourn." Perhaps, we have come not to the feet of a master, but a lunatic? This is not the case, however. Rather, it is our understanding of blessing, promise, and mourning that are askew, not the Master's. We tend to think only in terms of emotions, but mourning is a comprehensive part of all of our life. True mourning is concerned with much more than our initial emotional responses to the circumstances in which we find ourselves.

With mourning, there are both inward and outward forms. Inwardly, it is seeing our sinfulness. It's being poor in spirit and recognizing who God is and who we most certainly are not. Outwardly, we see how sin has ravaged the world: war, famine, poverty, racism, slavery, the list goes on . . . However, in this peculiar place of mourning, there is a blessing. Why? Because we see how incongruous our lives and our world are with Christ and his kingdom, but we see this knowing that Christ's kingdom is breaking into this world. There is a promise, and the promise of Christ's kingdom is a comfort to those who mourn. It's comforting in that what causes our mourning will one day be no more. Our sin will be no more, and all the devastating effects of sin in this world will be no more either.

Yet, this is also where the paradox exists. For, we know this kingdom that offers comfort is not yet fully here. It has begun to break in through Christ's life and ministry, but there is still so much to mourn. So, as faithful disciples, we must look to this beatitude with confidence, finding hope in the ways Christ already comforts our souls. We do so trusting in the promise of Christ's kingdom that is bringing about an unceasing and perfect comfort to our mourning.

What are you mourning, inwardly and outwardly? How does Christ give hope to our mourning? Have you accepted Christ's comfort, or do you tend to reject it and choose other forms of comfort?

Day 5: "Blessed are the meek, for they shall inherit the earth." (5:5)

THE TEMPTATION TO MISINTERPRET this beatitude is all too easy. We often read "meek" and think of weakness. Someone who is a pushover, or perhaps even someone who has a negative view of his or herself. We tend to think of meek in negative categories, rather than positive ones. However, this is not the idea at all. The idea of meekness is much more profound, and there is nothing negative about it, for Christ commends those who are meek. It does not mean that one must be some pitied creature, roaming about the earth eliciting the sympathy of others and in need of constant protection. Such a person may be vulnerable, but this is not necessarily a meek person.

Meekness is not a virtue for the poor or weak follower of Christ, it is a virtue for every follower of Christ. Meekness, in its truest sense, is actually about a peculiar type of strength. It is quiet strength. It is the type of strength that does not need to manifest itself through pride, arrogance, domineering, or violent behavior, but instead the type of strength that is in control, cool under pressure, and assesses oneself honestly and in light of God's holiness. Of course, the greatest example of meekness is displayed in Jesus' death on the cross.

Here we find the epitome of meekness, it is strength manifested through weakness: quiet strength. Jesus does not rebel, threaten, or try to escape the cross. He willingly submits to it by laying down his life, becoming weakened to the point of death, but in doing so he acts powerfully to save lost and wayward sinners. And this, Christian, is your call as well. To lay down power and prestige and take up your cross instead, becoming meek as Christ did to save others. It is sacrifice, humility, and gentleness unveiled through the courageous and bold act of allowing God's strength and fame to prevail over our own. Rather than exerting our strength or power, we rely on God. When we do so, we are meek as the Master calls us to be.

Where are you tempted to be prideful, to seek prestige, power, influence, or position? What will it look like for you to lay down the things that prevent meekness and take up your cross instead?

Day 6: "Blessed are those who hunger and thirst for righteousness, for they shall be satisfied." (5:6)

Jesus spoke these words to poor and oppressed people. They did not ask, "What will I eat for my next meal?" as we do, but rather, "will I be able to eat my next meal?" They possessed an intimate knowledge of hunger and thirst and experienced it in ways many of us never will. For them, the power of the metaphor Jesus used was not lost. In contrast, we have the luxury of restaurants on every corner, grocery stores, and bank accounts to purchase for our dietary needs. Whereas Jesus' audience lived day-to-day on subsistence farming. For many of Christ's disciples, each day was hand to mouth.

However, Jesus is not speaking about physical hunger here. He is speaking about spiritual hunger. So, if our spiritual needs can be compared to our physical need for food and water, how important must it be that our spiritual appetites are satisfied? Yet, how often are we content to let our spiritual lives dwindle, unfed and starving for the righteousness God has offered to us through his Son? Instead, we hunger and thirst for the blessings of this life rather than those of God. Thus, we find ourselves perpetually dissatisfied, unable to earn enough money, to feel that we have enough worth, to feel smart enough, or be pretty enough. Perhaps, we may find tiny glimmers of satisfaction from these things in this life. But in the end, we are left empty, starving for something more than this world offers.

The promise of this verse, however, is that there is satisfaction for those who hunger and thirst, and it is found by those who do so for the right thing: righteousness. Only then can we be satisfied, and that is because we find in Christ the eternal riches of righteousness that can completely fill our appetites. Through this we are filled again and again, healing our spiritual malnourishment, restoring us to life, and filling us with a righteousness that never leaves us hungry.

What are you truly hungry for? Is it Christ and his righteousness? If not, do you believe what you hunger for will truly satisfy you?

Day 7: "Blessed are the merciful, for they shall receive mercy." (5:7)

IN HIS CLASSIC WORK on community, *Life Together*, Dietrich Bonhoeffer writes these words, "Once a man has experienced the mercy of God in his life he will henceforth aspire only to serve. The proud throne of the judge no longer lures him; he wants to be down below with the lowly and the needy, because that is where God found him." How great is the gift of mercy? We may think of times when mercy has been extended to us and be reminded of how grateful we were, and even how such mercies changed our behavior for a time, perhaps.

The truth, however, is that as great as these mercies are, they pale in comparison to the mercy that God has offered to us in Christ. God's mercy is truly transformative. It doesn't simply change us for a moment of our lives but instead reorients us to a completely new way of living. In this way, the beatitude is actually somewhat backward. It's not that because we are merciful that God desires to show us mercy; this would be works-based righteousness that is inconsistent with the rest of Scripture. Rather, as followers of God, we have already received mercy for our sins and been forgiven through Christ's sacrifice, and this transforms our ways of interacting with others.

In contrast, think of the parable of the unforgiving servant (Matt 18:21-35). Here the servant is first extended mercy, yet his behavior is unchanged. He hasn't been transformed by the mercy and forgiveness that has been extended to him, but he instead goes and treats one of his own servants harshly. On the other hand, true mercy changes us and enables us to extend mercy as God has done to us. We do not act mercifully to receive God's mercy in exchange, but we are instead shaped into merciful people as we reflect on the great gift of mercy God has shown us in his Son.

Who are you withholding mercy from? How does God's mercy help us rethink what it is to be merciful to others? Are you harboring unforgiveness in your heart that you need to release?

Day 8: "Blessed are the pure in heart, for they shall see God." (5:8)

WE OFTEN SIMPLIFY THIS verse to the point that we make it an empty, legalistic manifesto. We see the word "pure" and speak of it only in terms of sexual purity. We forget that it is a purity of the *heart*, not just purity in our sexual conduct that is being discussed. When Jesus speaks of the heart, he is speaking of the whole person: heart, mind, soul, and body. It is all these constituent parts of the person that must be pure. We tend to limit Jesus' words and put them in a box we think we can manage. In reality, Jesus' words confront us on every level and do not fit nicely into the boxes we try to force them into.

Purity in heart means there is a wholeness to an individual, consistency throughout the thought, beliefs, motives, and actions of a person. It is a person who is unhypocritical and, by this, I do not only mean harmony between word and deed, but also belief and practice. It means a person is united in all that they do and all of what makes them who they are. When we begin to think of purity in such a way, we see that the Master's call is for much more than our sexual desires. It is, in fact, a call for our entire selves. That is what Jesus wants: every single bit of everything there is that makes us all of who we are. And Jesus will settle for nothing less.

But who could truly give all of themselves in this way? The truth is that we can't, but Christ has. Through his life we can also be pure in heart by his sacrifice and his righteousness. He took our sin, and in exchange we receive his purity in heart. All there is for us to do is to believe and give our lives to Christ, and when we give Christ our whole selves, we gain so much more than we ever give up. We can then truly see God. Our spiritual sight is opened, and we know God for who he truly is, and we can encounter him in the most intimate of ways.

In what ways do you need to seek purity? What parts of yourself are in conflict with others? How does Christ renew the brokenness and inconsistency of our lives?

Day 9: "Blessed are the peacemakers, for they shall be called sons of God." (5:9)

JESUS CALLS FOR HIS disciples to make peace, not to simply like the idea of peace or think of it as a concept we can accept or reject. Rather, Jesus presents it as a description of how his followers will be in this world. His followers are to be people who make peace. However, just as with much of the Sermon on the Mount, we tend to simplify the meaning. We hear peace and think of a world without war or violence, and one in which people are friendly and get along. True, this is indeed an aspect of peace. But just as with the previous beatitude, this surface-level reading is certainly not the whole meaning.

Jesus' use of the word peace is rooted in the context of the Hebrew word found in the Old Testament for peace, *shalom*. This is what Jesus is speaking about. It is the idea of universal wholeness, completeness of being, a world in which everything is as it should be, as God intended it to be. Relationships between ourselves, God, creation, and others are in harmony with one another. Shalom means that the systems and policies that undergird our society provide flourishing for all. Shalom, in its truest sense, is God dwelling among humanity, just as the prophets foretold in the Old Testament and which we see fulfilled in Christ.

After all, is this not the picture we see when we look to the final pages of Scripture? We see God right there in the midst of the new creation alongside his redeemed people, the Church! There are no tears, pain, or hate. No one is hungry, sick, or broken. It is whole, it is shalom, it is peace. This is the kingdom that Christ is talking about in the Sermon! And this kingdom is breaking into every day right here and right now. When we live as peacemakers, we are truly living as citizens of his kingdom, as children of the living God and ambassadors of the heavenly realm.

> *Where do you need to make peace in your life? With yourself, or with others? Where does the church need to make peace in or with the rest of the world? Where do we already see the shalom of God's kingdom here on earth?*

Day 10: "Blessed are those who are persecuted for righteousness'
sake, for theirs is the kingdom of heaven." (5:10)

IF ANY OF THE beatitudes flies in the face of modern, Western Christianity,
it is this one. We may think that we would follow Christ to any extent but,
certainly, that must not entail persecution! However, Christian, this is your
calling as a follower and disciple of Christ. It is to bear the same burdens
Christ experienced. It is to take up your cross and follow Jesus, whether
that results in the call to lay down your life or to graciously bear the brunt
of insults and being an outcast in society. It is to face negative treatment
simply because of who you are in Christ.

But we are also aware of what this beatitude is not. It is not about being
persecuted for a political belief, being unpleasant and intolerable, or for
having persecuted others. Nor is it suggesting that you are persecuted because you did not get your way. It only speaks of persecution that is a result
of suffering for "righteousness' sake." That is the only premise in which the
beatitude allows for persecution to be a blessing.

The promise that is attached to this beatitude echoes the first (Matt
5:3). It is to receive the Kingdom of Heaven, which is what all the beatitudes are promising by describing various manifestations of the kingdom
(i.e., comfort, inheriting the earth, mercy, etc.). This penultimate beatitude is telling us what marks true citizens of the kingdom: it is to be poor
in spirit, meek, mournful, pure, and merciful; makers of peace who pursue righteousness and are in turn persecuted for the very things they seek.
Yet, it is these who gain the kingdom.

Like one who feels the physical pangs of hunger, so will the true citizen
perpetually long for righteousness. It is they who will search for joy amid
their own persecution, knowing that the promises of the kingdom are coming. The eternal is colliding with the now, and the promises are coming true
in the present. The kingdom is on the move! And though the kingdom's
citizens may suffer today, glory awaits. That glory will make the strife of this
life seem utterly inconsequential compared to the blessings found when
we, Christ's Church, dwell for eternity with God. That, my friends, is the
kingdom we suffer for now to gain in the future.

*What are you persecuted for? Is it righteousness, or for something
else? Do you ever persecute others? Does Christ's kingdom make the
persecutions you face today seem more trivial or not?*

Day 11: "Blessed are you when others revile you and persecute you and utter all kinds of evil against you falsely on my account." (5:11)

JESUS IS NOW BEING explicit. All the beatitudes have been building up, one upon the other, and now they culminate in the persecution that is sure to occur from following Christ. There are no more broad truths being proclaimed in the beatitudes. Instead, an intentional turn is made here by the Master. It's personal now. Previously, Jesus has been speaking in larger concepts about what the kingdom looks like. Now he applies the beatitudes directly to his disciples, telling them what results from following the Master and living out the kingdom.

Likewise, if we are followers of Christ, we can imagine ourselves in this position. We, too, are sitting at the feet of the Master who instructs us on how to live as citizens of the kingdom. It means that we must embody the beatitudes in our lives as well. Not because this will make us true followers of Christ. Rather, since we are followers of Christ, we aspire to the call to live in a particular manner. This means we may also suffer persecution because of Christ as the disciples did. It means others may utter evil things about us, slander us, and speak maliciously about us because we live lives that mimic the beatitudes. This is what it means to live like a heavenly citizen in this world. We are living against the grain, inviting Christ's eternal principles into our present lives. Therefore, we may face persecution by following Christ as well.

Despite this, we must always remember that if we are rejected, we are not alone. When rejected, we are in the company of Christ, "If the world hates you, know that it has hated me before it hated you. If you were of the world, the world would love you as its own; but because you are not of the world, but I chose you out of the world, therefore the world hates you" (John 15:18-19). Take comfort, my friends. Our persecutions, though difficult, only bring us closer to Christ.

Why does the Christian life call for persecution? Are you being persecuted for Christ's sake, or for some other reason? How might we be sure we are persecuted for Christ's sake, and not for our own or any other reason?

Day 12: "Rejoice and be glad, for your reward is great in heaven, for so they persecuted the prophets who were before you." (5:12)

WHEN THE PROMISE OF heaven is before us, the persecutions of this life become exceedingly insignificant. They may still exist, and they may still hurt both physically and emotionally, but they lose their power as they fail to be relevant to the overall trajectory of life when one is following Christ. The disciple of Christ is bound for the eternal Kingdom of Heaven, and this life and its woes are merely temporary.

Thus, as followers of Christ, we are to rejoice. We are to give God joyful praise, knowing that he will not let this present life win in the end but, instead, will bring about his rule on earth. In fact, this is what it means to be a part of God's people. It is to seek God's kingdom here on earth. When we do, we will come face to face with persecution just as the prophets did so long ago. As they sought to pursue the kingdom, they called Israel to righteousness and, as a result, they were persecuted.

You see, friend, the reason is this: God's kingdom is entirely different from the world in which we live. It is a kingdom of peace, whereas this world seeks to embrace violence. It is a kingdom of justice, while this world is content to oppress and exploit. It is a kingdom of love while this world is content to harbor hate and disunity. When we seek these things, these characteristics of the kingdom, we are living against the grain of this world. We are like a fish swimming upstream, facing the torrents of life that would have us give up the prize and be swept away with the current.

But, Christian, this must not be so! Not for you, not for me, and not for the Church. We must seek first the kingdom, knowing that glory awaits our journey and pursuit of God's kingdom. When we encounter persecution, we must look heavenward again, knowing that God is working to make his kingdom present here on earth. When we are reminded that the kingdom is coming, we have every reason to be glad and to rejoice.

Are you tempted to become discouraged when you face persecution? What are appropriate ways to rejoice amid persecution? What may be inappropriate ways of rejoicing and being glad during persecution?

Day 13: "You are the salt of the earth, but if salt has lost its taste, how shall its saltiness be restored? It is no longer good for anything except to be thrown out and trampled under people's feet." (5:13)

JESUS USES SALT AS a metaphor because it is unique, it is distinct. It stands out among all other flavors and is immediately recognizable in a dish. Too much, and the dish is ruined. Too little, and the dish is bland and unappetizing. That is the power of salt. Its distinctiveness is so powerful that it can completely alter a meal for better or worse. This, my friend, is true of anyone who claims to follow Christ as well.

The Christian must be such a person that they are immediately recognizable. Among all the other people in the world, Christians must stand out as distinct and unique. This is what our Master is calling us to in the Sermon on the Mount, and this is what it means to be Christ's Church. He is giving us the recipe, so to speak, for how we may be kingdom citizens, standing out among the mélange of competing worldviews and ethical systems that this life has to offer. Where the world tastes bland the Christian must add flavor by living as a heavenly citizen. Not overpowering to the point of being unbearable, but subtly altering the flavor such that those who come into contact with Christians see how they enhance the world through their pursuit of Christ and by obeying his commands.

However, with the call to live as salt, there is also the stern warning that Christians must not lose their unique flavor. They must be ever flavorful in a world that would have them become dull or diluted by the other flavors in the world. When this occurs, as Jesus tells us, the Christian has become useless, they have failed to heed the call of the Sermon. Therefore, my brothers and sisters, we must purposefully pursue Christ, daily answering the beckoning call of Christ's sermon so that our lives are flavorful and distinct. By the Holy Spirit, may our lives be full of flavor!

In what ways are you tempted to become dull and less flavorful?
In what ways has God uniquely gifted you to be salt in this world?
Where have we, the Church, lost our flavor and how do we regain it?

Day 14: "You are the light of the world. A city
set on a hill cannot be hidden." (5:14)

LIKE SALT, LIGHT IS also a powerful metaphor. However, in our modern world of electricity, we have perhaps lost the power of Christ's language. The disciples lived in a time without a vast power grid to light up the sky at any given moment. They lived in a day-to-day routine that was clearly marked by whether the sun was up or down, there was daylight and there was darkness. Though their day-to-day life was ultimately dependent on sunlight, cities did still emit noticeable light during the night.

Imagine it for a second. In your mind, go back to a time long before electricity. You find yourself outside of a city when the sun has gone down. You are surrounded by darkness, there is hardly any ambient light, save what is available from the moon and stars, and you cannot see more than what is immediately before you. How would you navigate? How would you know how to make your way home? You scan the horizon and only a small speck of light is visible, but that small speck is, in fact, the city from which you have come. Surrounded by nothing but inescapable darkness, there is indeed a light that can provide guidance and lead you home! There is no other direction to turn but homeward, towards the speck of light which is the only distinguishable thing in sight.

So too must the Christian be. Amid the darkness of this world, the Christian must shine, providing a guiding light to those lost in the darkness. We shine by obeying Christ's words in the Sermon and, when we do so, we light the way so that others may find their way to God. Across the dark landscape, we must be illuminating, a people marked and set apart by our obedience to God and his Word. We must live in such a way so that others are drawn to God by the way we live our lives. Like an ancient city lit up by fiery lanterns, the words of Christ's sermon must also light up the life of the Master's disciples, providing the welcoming call for others to come and follow Christ.

*Would you say that you offer a bright light or a dull light? How so?
How may Christ's words in the Sermon transform your life so that
you may shine more brightly?*

Day 15: "Nor do people light a lamp and put it under a basket, but on a stand, and it gives light to all in the house." (5:15)

THIS MAY SEEM OBVIOUS, but light is intended to illuminate what is dark. We can safely assume that Jesus states these words because some claim to follow him, yet do not shine as light does. However, light is only capable of shining. Light cannot choose to not shine. It is meant to shine, enabling us to see the form, color, and attributes of the world that surround us. It is meant to give clarity to what is obscure, piercing through the darkness, so that what is hidden may be made known.

Furthermore, light is essential to life. Without light, our earth would be a cold and barren rock, floating through the solar system lifelessly and without inhabitants. However, when light is present, so is life in all the diverse forms that make up this world. Just as light has a purpose, so does the Christian. The Christian is meant to shine, bringing clarity to a confusing world by proclaiming the life that God has offered to us through his Son. The Christian has the God-ordained purpose of piercing through the darkness of this age, making visible the edges, form, color, and shape of the kingdom.

As I've said before, my friends, it is by embracing the words of Christ's sermon, and seeking to live it out, that we shine as Christ desires. When the beatitudes become our way of living in this world, then we will truly shine. Then we will have the luminosity that Christ desires of his disciples. But we must always be wary, for the temptation to withhold the light of Christ is ever-present. It is present because we know that Jesus' earlier warnings of persecution are real, and if we embrace the call of the Sermon, we will face persecution. But, dear friend, though there may be persecution, we must remember that light always prevails. It does not fail, just as John's Gospel reminds us, "The light shines in the darkness, and the darkness has not overcome it." (John 1:5)

Do you display or conceal your light? How so? At what times and moments are you tempted to conceal the light of Christ, and how may you live in such a way that allows your light to shine in this world?

Day 16: "In the same way, let your light shine before others, so that they may see your good works and give glory to your Father who is in heaven." (5:16)

THE CHRISTIAN CANNOT CONCEAL the light they have. This is a crucial aspect of following the Master and his teachings. If we fail to grasp this fact, then we will live a life of vanities filled with perpetually empty moments that we think will gratify ourselves. In the end, however, they are hollow experiences that only leave us wanting. Why? Well, the answer is twofold.

First, it is because when we fail to shine our light we are not living as our Creator has designed us to live. We are not embracing the life that is offered to us in Christ and letting this life be on display. When we fail in this first regard, we should not be surprised if our lives feel meaningless, as if we are simply meandering through life without purpose. It is because we are neglecting what we are created to do. Instead, we are trying to satisfy our desires by living some lesser life than we are called to, yet still expecting to find purpose within it. Secondly, we are left wanting when we fail to shine our light because we lose focus on who we are living for. When we do not shine the light of Christ we focus inwardly, looking only at ourselves and the things that concern us. We lose sight of the world around us, forgetting that our call to follow Christ is equally a call to serve and bless those around us.

We are called to shine our light so that others may see and glorify God. It's not about you at all, my friend! It is about living in such a way that others are drawn to God by the way you live, resulting in those around you glorifying God by seeking to live similarly, joining in the pursuit of Christ. Only then will we live with the purpose to which God has called us. The question is, knowing this, why would we try to settle for anything less than this?

Do you feel that your life has meaning? Do you feel like your life brings you fulfillment? If not, have you tried living in the way that Jesus instructs?

Day 17: "Do not think that I have come to abolish the Law or the Prophets; I have not come to abolish them but to fulfill them." (5:17)

SINCE THE EARLIEST DAYS of Christianity, there has been the temptation to separate the Old and New Testaments, to see them as wholly removed from one another and as separate collections of books that do not bear upon one another. In fact, this was one of the earliest heresies the Christian church faced in history. Jesus himself says, "By no means!" to getting rid of the Old Testament. Though there is a distinction between the two testaments, there is no division.

Jesus is not saying to do away with the Old Testament but, rather, is showing how the Old Testament comes to fruition. A fuller sense of the Old Testament writings is now found in the person of Christ. He does not see himself as a rebel breaking away from Jewish tradition to create a new faith and religion. Instead, Jesus is bringing the promises of the Old Testament to completion. He is fulfilling what the law spoke of and whom the prophets spoke about. He does not render it useless, pitch it to the side and call it irrelevant, or relativize it to obscurity. No, he fulfills it! He brings it to bear and he makes it complete. To put it simply, he does it. He lives what the laws require and fulfills what the prophets have spoken of for so long, and this should change our perspective on the Old Testament entirely.

It is not simply a set of rules with some hollow promises but, instead, is the living and active Word found in the work and person of Jesus Christ. What perhaps before seemed stale, demanding, and irrelevant comes to life as we recognize that, when we read the Old Testament, Jesus is staring us in the face as we read each page. Christ brings life to the Old Testament through his life and ministry, taking caution to demonstrate that God's Word from old prevails in his life. Therefore, we must read it knowing it finds its clearest portrayal in Christ. So, friends, may we be encouraged to see Christ in all of Scripture, knowing that he is the sure and true fulfillment of it all.

Do you have an aversion to the Old Testament? If so, why? How does Christ make us better readers of the Old Testament?

Day 18: "For truly, I say to you, until heaven and earth pass away, not an iota, not a dot, will pass from the Law until all is accomplished." (5:18)

THE WORD OF GOD stands, and Jesus does not waver on this point one bit. He intentionally makes it clear that what God has spoken and promised will not go unfulfilled. Jesus is ensuring that his audience is well aware that there is a continuity between the words he speaks in the Sermon and what God had spoken long ago through the prophets and Old Testament writers. As we saw yesterday, Jesus fulfills the Old Testament. He does not discard it, and the reason is that it is a part of God's enduring revelation that persists throughout time.

We must also note, when Jesus speaks of the "law," we may hear his words incorrectly. We perhaps think of judges and courts, but Jesus' reference to the law is found in the Old Testament concept of Torah: meaning teaching or instruction. It is a covenantal term for establishing the relationship between God and his people. There are boundaries and restrictions for the relationship to be maintained, but they are not some set of arbitrary commands to control behavior. They are in place so that the people of God may flourish in their relationship with God and each other. This is the law that Jesus is saying must be accomplished, and Jesus is the fulfiller of this law. Therefore, the law cannot pass away into obscurity because it is embodied in who Jesus is.

So, we must see that the words of the Sermon are pointing out how the law is being accomplished. Jesus is the perfect example of the law and he is the perfect example of the Sermon. By this, we know what it means to truly be followers of God and fulfillers of the law. It is to live by his instruction and teaching, and we do so as we invite the teachings of the Sermon into our lives. As we do so, we too embody God's enduring law. Of course, this law does not save us or offer us salvation, that only occurs through Christ. But, since we are citizens of Christ's heavenly kingdom, we live according to the King's decrees.

Does it sometimes seem easier to just abandon the Old Testament and only pay attention to the New? What would Jesus say about this? How does Jesus help us look for a better relationship with God through the law?

Day 19: "Therefore whoever relaxes one of the least of these commandments and teaches others to do the same will be called least in the kingdom of heaven, but whoever does them and teaches them will be called great in the kingdom of heaven." (5:19)

JESUS TAKES HIS WORD seriously. He does not deal in ambiguities or allow for surface-level readings that waffle on the applications of the Sermon. Not at all. Jesus puts it clearly before us. The Master tells us exactly what he requires of those who learn at his feet and are called his disciples. They are to be doers of the words that Jesus speaks. They are not to relax, negate, or lessen the severity of anything he speaks, but are instead to embrace Christ's words and live by them.

Not only this, but Christ also calls his disciples to teach these precepts to others and to do so because the Kingdom of Heaven is at stake. The disciple of Christ is called into radical obedience, following Christ closely and seeking to live on earth now as a citizen of Christ's heavenly kingdom. This does not mean that everything in the Sermon is to be taken literally (e.g. cutting out your eye or cutting off your hand), as Jesus commonly speaks in hyperbole to emphasize his point. What it does mean is that we must fervently search for the truth the Master is conveying and, once that is found, we embrace it wholeheartedly and live by it. No questions asked. If Jesus tells us not to lust, think evil thoughts, or to covet, then we do not do such things. If Jesus tells us to give generously, love our enemies, and pray for those who persecute us, then we do so as well. We do not relativize these points to obscurity, but joyfully assent to what our Lord requires.

When we do this, we will find that the Sermon makes a claim on our entire lives. There is no part of us left untouched and unfazed by Christ's words. He goes to the core, seeking to transform us from the inside out and, when we follow his teaching, we find that our lives will look drastically different. That is because we are no longer living as citizens of this earthly world, but as citizens of Christ's kingdom. Doing so means we look distinctively different from the rest of the world. To use Christ's own words, we look like salt and light in a world that is bland and dark.

Are you tempted to minimize Christ's teachings, or to suggest that we shouldn't take them as seriously as he suggests? Are you obeying, as well as teaching, Christ's words?

Day 20: "For I tell you, unless your righteousness exceeds that of the scribes and Pharisees, you will never enter the kingdom of heaven." (5:20)

THE SCRIBES AND THE Pharisees were among the religious elite in ancient Judaism. They were not only the interpreters and teachers of the law, but were also seen as those who upheld the law. They were the moral exemplars of what Torah living looked like for many ancient Jews. However, Jesus seems to think they have missed out on a crucial aspect of what the Law and the prophets were teaching.

This is exactly what Jesus is going to discuss next in the Sermon, and it will unfold over the next 28 verses. The Master is going to lay out what this higher standard of righteousness, that exceeds that of the scribes and Pharisees, looks like. We may be tempted to think that the Pharisees existed only in ancient times, but we would be wise to recognize that their notions of upholding the law for salvation are pervasive in the Church today. We too often believe in works-based righteousness, or legalism, suggesting that we can earn God's favor by doing this or that, or not doing something or the other. The truth is this form of works-based righteousness is an insult to the grace God has offered us in Jesus Christ.

So, what then of these commands that Christ gives us to live by? Do we scrap them? Not at all! As Christians, it is only by God's grace that we can even hope to live by them. These are commands for Christ's disciples, those who are bought and purchased by his blood and redeemed by his death and resurrection. It is through Christ's work that we may be filled with the Holy Spirit and empowered to live out Christ's teaching. Though we will not get it perfect, we strive daily to embrace Christ's words. Christ is the true perfecter of the Sermon, so we follow him by taking up our own cross and living obediently. When Christ's kingdom is fully established, then we may truly live out the Sermon. But, until then, we invite the eternal into our everyday living so that we may live as Christ's disciples and members of his kingdom in the present.

Are you tempted to live by works-based righteousness, striving to earn God's favor, grace, and mercy? How does the Sermon call us to better, truer righteousness than legalism?

Day 21: "You have heard that it was said to those of old, 'You shall not murder; and whoever murders will be liable to judgment.'" (5:21)

THIS COMMAND SEEMS EASY enough, "do not murder." We might think, "Got it! I'm not guilty of this one and can move on." However, to think like this is to ignore what Christ is going to go on and say about murder. To think like this is to think as the Pharisees did, believing if they simply did not literally take another person's life that they are innocent of murder. Now, such thinking may hold up in the court of law, but it does not hold up in the Kingdom of Heaven.

The Kingdom of Heaven requires holiness, and that means every part of a person must be innocent of murder, including the heart. It means that no thought of ill-will, hate, or murder, is a part of our thinking or desires. We may easily get discouraged here, thinking that we have already violated the intention of the command, and we have. Afterall, who could actually live up to this standard of righteousness? Remember, as I've stated before, Jesus Christ is the true perfecter of the Sermon. He has fulfilled the words he speaks within it, thereby demonstrating his righteousness. And, by God's grace through faith, we have received Christ's righteousness. This does not mean that we are then free to abandon Christ's teachings, but it means that we approach them with loving obedience. It means that we, filled with the Holy Spirit, strive to live up to the holy standards of the Sermon each day.

This command of Christ goes immediately to the core of the Old Testament, to love your neighbor as yourself (Lev 19:18). Christ fulfills this command by not punishing guilty sinners to death but, rather, dying in their place that they may have life. My dear brothers and sisters, we must be ever mindful of this command and seek to live in accordance with it. The temptation to murder is all too easy, and it fills our hearts daily. So, seek Christ and live by his example, which does not harm others but dies in their place instead.

Is there murder in your heart of which you need to repent? How might our hearts be full of love and life for others instead of hate and murder?

Day 22: "But I say to you that everyone who is angry with his brother will be liable to judgment; whoever insults his brother will be liable to the council; and whoever says, 'You fool!' will be liable to the hell of fire." (5:22)

HERE WE SEE JESUS go to the heart of the matter concerning murder, and he does so with an interesting rhetorical technique. As he speaks, there are simultaneous de-escalations and escalations taking place. The first part of the phrase de-escalates: anger, then insult, and then calling someone a "fool." They descend in order of severity. The word for anger denotes a very vivid image, the type of anger that is associated with wrath. The word for "insult" in the biblical text is *rhaka*, a word found only once in the New Testament. The idea behind it is that someone is worthless, empty, and lacking any value. Finally, the one who calls someone a "fool," a somewhat common and generic insult in the New Testament, appearing around a dozen times in the New Testament. The movement is from wrathful rage to something like a curse word, and then to a common insult, showing a pattern that we might think of as decreasing in severity.

Alongside this decrease in transgression is the increase in resulting punishment: judgment, the council, and finally the "hell of fire." This move demonstrates an escalation in severity, with the end result being the final judgment. However, it is paired with what we may think is the least offensive of the three transgressions: calling someone a "fool." The purpose of this device is to demonstrate that they are all in parallel with one another. It does not matter the crime. If hate, in any form, is in your heart, on your lips, or on your hands, then you are guilty. All expressions of hate fall under the category and decree not to murder. Jesus is demonstrating how deadly even the slightest word of hate can be. The old adage, "sticks and stones may break my bones, but words will never hurt me" doesn't hold up for Jesus. Not only will the words we speak to someone else destroy them and bring them down, but they also destroy our very selves when we think and speak in such ways. Brothers and sisters, I beg you, weigh your words carefully! We must be certain that our speech mimics that of Christ, building each other up in love and without a trace of hate or anger.

When are you tempted to bring someone down with either angry or hateful speech? How might you, with the help of the Holy Spirit, work to better tame your anger, temper, and spoken words?

Day 23: "So if you are offering your gift at
the altar and there remember that your brother
has something against you . . ." (5:23)

How often, brothers and sisters, do we come to worship with hate in our
hearts? Maybe our anger is the result of simply getting ready in the morning
and driving to church, or perhaps an unreconciled dispute between husband
and wife? Or, as this verse suggests, downright enmity between ourselves
and a fellow believer? How often are we content to come and worship still
harboring malice towards another person? Jesus says this cannot be. In fact,
he even states that our lives as worshippers and the relationships we have
with others cannot be separated from one another.

Let's stop. Pause for a moment right now. Is there anyone in your life
that needs your forgiveness, or whose forgiveness you need? Is there anything lingering, no matter how trivial, that is left unresolved? My friend, let it
not be so! Go now and be reconciled! Don't spend another moment trying to
come before God if anything is preventing you from coming before another
brother or sister in Christ. Jesus desires that our relationships be whole, un-
defiled and healthy—and it is when our relationships are in such a state that
we can best come before the Lord in worship. Certainly, from time to time,
we are at odds with one another. But this must not prevail, as we who have
been forgiven by God must be ever ready to forgive others.

Isn't that the greatest source of our Christian union, as well? That we
are bonded together through Christ's death and resurrection, through the
forgiveness of our sins? If this is the basis for our unity with one another,
shouldn't it be an essential element of our relationships with one another
as well? We cannot allow disunity in any regard, rather, we must always
be able to approach each other as reconciled believers. Reconciled both to
God and to one another. Dear Christian, this allows no room for brood-
ing on past wrongs. We must be willing to forgive, but also ready to seek
forgiveness when we are at fault. There is no option for self-justification of
our wrongs and no allowance to withhold forgiveness, but only room for
the peace and forgiveness of Christ to prevail.

*Is there anyone with whom you need to seek reconciliation? What
prevents you from seeking reconciliation with others? If there is a
reason, is it better than our unity in Christ?*

Day 24: ". . . leave your gift there before the altar and
go. First be reconciled to your brother, and
then come and offer your gift." (5:24)

FORGIVENESS AND RECONCILIATION REQUIRE an initial step, they need action. Yet, this is also our greatest hindrance when it comes to finding reconciliation. We are unwilling to admit that we have done wrong. This is one of our most natural inclinations: to believe that we are without error and that every broken relationship in our lives is the result of someone else's actions. Thus, we do not feel the burden to mend the broken relationship.

My friends, when we do this, it breaks Christ's heart. He desires that his church be one and united, just as he prayed moments before his trial and execution: "I do not ask for these only, but also for those who will believe in me through their word, that they may all be one, just as you, Father, are in me, and I in you. . ." (John 17:20-21a). Christ longs for his followers to live in harmony with one another. Yet, we still let so many petty differences drive us apart. Whether it be politics, worship practices, or minor dogmas, we easily let these things create barriers of hostility, rather than moving beyond them so that we might be the type of church that Christ prayed we would be. Our pride gets in the way. So, we must instead embrace the humility and meekness of the Master if we hope to live as Christ longs for us to live. We must look at our lives and determine what broken relationships we bring to the altar that we have not reconciled.

What unforgiveness, on your part or another's, is in your life that you bring to the altar but haven't let go of yet? Let me point out, according to this verse, whatever it is you may be clinging onto is in fact what prevents you from coming before God to worship. Brothers and sisters, let these things go! Be reconciled to each other, forgive wholly and sacrificially, walk in humility, and do whatever it takes so that peace may reign in your life and the lives of those around you. Christ longs desperately for this.

*Is there bitterness or unforgiveness in your life that you have not let
go? If so, why? Does Christ's heart for his church to be one allow you
the option to not forgive another, or to not seek forgiveness?*

Day 25: "Come to terms quickly with your accuser while you are going with him to court, lest your accuser hand you over to the judge, and the judge to the guard, and you be put in prison." (5:25)

WE HAVE ALL BEEN accused of something at some point in our lives. Whether that accusation was correct or incorrect, we have all felt the sting of an outstretched finger pointing our direction, calling out our errors. In this verse, the text seems to imply that the accusation is correct, and the one accused truly deserves the punishment that awaits. However, Jesus calls for reconciliation that works in both directions. It works in us to forgive those who have wronged us and for us to seek forgiveness from those we have wronged.

As we read yesterday, we must not let our pride get in the way of this. Why? Notice what is at risk. Due judgment awaits those who are unwilling to seek reconciliation with their accusers. This may seem harsh, but this is the reality that Christ's words present to us. We must also remember that at many times in our lives we stand rightly accused. Now, that may be discouraging, but we must also remember how Christ's life transforms our understanding of the Sermon. Though Christ has every right to point the accusing finger at us, he instead laid down his life on our behalf. Though Christ possesses the authority to hand us over to condemnation, we may come to him in faith so that we do not face the judgment we rightly deserve: "For by grace you have been saved through faith. And this is not your own doing; it is the gift of God, not a result of works, so that no one may boast" (Eph 2:8-9).

Here we see the great benefit of reconciliation: it is salvation and redemption. We can experience a smaller picture of this when we seek to come to terms with those who accuse us. We can find life in a relationship that once was dead. We can find hope in a dismal situation that seems irreconcilable. We can find restoration of what we previously thought was unmendable. Friend, we paint a picture of the gospel when we do this, declaring with our lives that broken relationships can be made whole. We do this because Christ commands it of us and because he has truly shown us what it means for a relationship to be reconciled.

Are there accusers in your life now? If so, are their accusations correct? What steps may need to be taken by you, not them, to bring about reconciliation?

Day 26: "Truly, I say to you, you will never get out until you have paid the last penny." (5:26)

THE FACT THAT GOD is just flies in the face of our modern Western culture. Any assertion that God would punish wickedness and evil is unpalatable to our contemporary notions of an all-loving God who is benevolent in all things. Ironically, though, the passage here is not talking about God's judgment at all. It's talking about the idea of retribution between two individuals, something with which we don't normally have a problem at all. If I damage your property or cause you some sort of loss, I make amends for it. We get this, and it really isn't a struggle for us to come to terms with.

Yet, when it is God who desires justice for wrongdoing and ill in the world, suddenly it becomes a problem. We want parity and equanimity in our own relationships, but we think God must lay justice aside when it comes to sin. Certainly, a loving God would be willing to excuse any and all evil at no cost? God is indeed merciful and forgiving, but we often forget that he is equally just. With God, sin is either mercifully forgiven through Christ, or rightfully punished in justice. God does indeed offer mercy and forgiveness to all, but they certainly are not free.

Once again, we have the question of reconciliation before us, and again it is Christ who offers us a true picture of this. Though we deserve condemnation that must be paid to the "last penny," we do not have to make that payment since Christ has paid it in full. Because of this, we know what forgiveness truly is, and we can be a people who seek to forgive and be forgiven. Truly, it is the Christian who knows forgiveness best. We have each felt the weight of sin lifted from us and have experienced the pardon of forgiveness. Therefore, it is we who should be most known by forgiveness. It should be at the center of all our relationships. As forgiveness has transformed us from the inside out, so too must it be a transforming power in our earthly relationships. Never forget this! You have been forgiven by God and, therefore, you have an intimate knowledge of forgiveness. Be certain that it is always evident in all of your relationships as well.

How does Christ's forgiveness change the way we interact with others? Why are we often so hesitant to forgive despite how much Christ has forgiven us?

Day 27: "You have heard that it was said, 'You shall not commit adultery.'" (5:27)

LET ME BEGIN BY saying that the warning to flee adultery is no small one. With haunting regularity, we see great men and women, Christian and non-Christian alike, succumb to the temptation to betray their marital vows. Though the stories may live in the headlines for a short while, they are soon forgotten until the next incidence comes along. What we don't see, however, is the years of anguish, hurt, and damage that are the result of adultery. In my own family, I have seen this before, and a type of loss is created by adulterous relationships that can never be fully recovered. Things cannot return to the way they were before, and although forgiveness and reconciliation may be achieved, there is an aspect to all the relationships involved that is affected which does not fully mend.

The ramifications of adultery are indeed vast, and the number of people affected by a single incident of infidelity can be massive. Furthermore, there is a crucial theological principle at stake within Christian marriages: the gospel itself. The Christian marriage is meant to proclaim the gospel, the story of God's love and redemption of his bride, the Church (Eph 5:31-32). When adultery enters a Christian marriage, it mars the good news that we hope to proclaim. It is no different than Christ's church seeking after other gods, making idols of things which are not God at all, and being wed to falseness instead of truth. Adultery is the proclamation of a false gospel, where we declare that our ways are better than God's and that our desires reign supreme over Christ's calling for us in marriage.

In light of this, we can see the high calling that it is to marry. It is so high that God is even willing to stake his name on it and allow us to declare his redemptive love through our most intimate relationships. Brothers and sisters, be fully devoted in your marriage and be true, knowing that how you live in marriage reflects the profound mystery of God redeeming his bride, the Church, through his Son.

> *Have we become content with adultery in our society? In what ways does adultery mar the proclamation of the gospel? What might we do to prevent any hint of adultery from entering our own marriages? If you are single, how can you support the marriages of those around you?*

Day 28: "But I say to you that everyone who looks at a woman with lustful intent has already committed adultery with her in his heart." (5:28)

JESUS JUST CAN'T LET good enough alone. He just has to raise the stakes for his disciples. Rather than simply affirming what the Old Testament already teaches, he takes it a step further. The one who looks lustfully at another is guilty of adultery as well, not just those who engage in the physical act. Why does Jesus introduce such a standard? Doesn't it seem well beyond what Scripture already teaches? Well, it may seem so, but we must remember that Christ is calling for the transformation of his disciples from the inside out. Jesus is not only concerned with the acts that we do but also our motivations and intentions; Jesus is concerned about our hearts. Outward appearances of piety are simply not enough.

So, here, to follow the Master and his teaching means abandoning any desires that keep us from God, whether or not those desires are acted upon. We must be whole, complete people. To follow Christ in this manner means that we no longer covet and envy that which is not ours. It means that our hearts must be transformed in such a way that they are oriented towards God entirely, undeterred by the temptations of this world. And, as we read yesterday, this is because so much is at stake in marriage. The gospel is on display in our marriages, and the slightest hint of infidelity proclaims a faulty and broken gospel.

Friends, let us then fix our eyes upon our Messiah instead of fleshly desires. Give him your heart entirely and let him possess every ounce of your devotion. Do not seek to consume others with your eyes, as the Master has told us this is sinful, and it corrupts our very hearts. We cannot be deceived, thinking that we can harmlessly gawk at others. We must not let our hearts desire that which is not our own or desire things in inappropriate ways. Instead, we must allow our gaze to rest solely upon Christ. Christian, be mindful of where your eyes go, knowing that our eyes must seek what pleases God.

In what ways are you guilty of violating Christ's command, and what might repentance look like? How might we be better stewards of our eyes, not looking upon things in such a way that dishonors God?

Day 29: "If your right eye causes you to sin, tear it out and throw it away. For it is better that you lose one of your members than that your whole body be thrown into hell." (5:29)

HERE WE SEE THE severity with which Jesus discusses adultery. It is not a matter of some inconsequential sin that we can simply brush under the rug, it is a matter of heaven and hell. Now, we might be tempted to take these verses too literally, so we must recognize that Jesus is using hyperbole. The Master is not telling us to actually disfigure our bodies so that we may not lust. Rather, Jesus is pointing out how serious the sin of adultery is, and how costly are its ramifications.

We too must embrace the same concern as Christ in the matter. If there is anything in our lives that leads to the sin of adultery, we must remove it from our lives. This includes the types of entertainment we choose to watch, the books we read, or the websites we visit. If they create lustful intent in our hearts, we must rid them from our lives. Jesus is telling us that if there is anything that would separate us from the Kingdom of Heaven, it must be discarded immediately. It is far better that we seek his kingdom broken than to have our bodies whole and forsake it altogether. This means that we must be ever-conscious of what is in our lives that may lead us to sin. Though this passage is referring to the sin of lust, it could be just as easily applied to pride, envy, jealousy, malice, anger, and so on. Whatever it may be, we must be willing to forsake it to gain the kingdom.

My friend, we must then consider what it is that stirs up the desires in our hearts. Is it lusting after another person, or is it seeking Christ and his kingdom? Do we find our joy in satisfying our own fleshly appetites, or in pursuing God's will and desire for our lives? These are indeed serious questions, so we must take note of the severity of the issue. The Kingdom of Heaven and judgment are at stake, and we cannot have our sin and the kingdom at the same time. It is only one or the other.

What do you need to remove from your life to address lustful intentions you have? What makes it so difficult to remove these things from our lives? Does Christ's teaching change the way you think and relate to these things?

Day 30: "And if your right hand causes you to sin, cut it off and throw it away. For it is better that you lose one of your members than that your whole body go into hell." (5:30)

IN CASE WE MISSED it the first time, Jesus makes it abundantly clear here. You cannot have the kingdom and your sin at the same time. You cannot be driven solely by your desires and claim the Kingdom of God as your own. Because, when our lives are driven by lustful desire, we have declared that what we desire takes precedence before the kingdom. We have made an idol of something other than the living God of Scripture, and we have allowed whatever that thing may be to rule over us instead of the King of the universe.

Unfortunately, this is our tendency. As John Calvin put it, "man's nature is a perpetual factory of idols," always creating a new object to worship rather than the Creator. We do this when we lust after other individuals, hoping to take them as our own. However, we soon find out that we have made something else lord over our lives. Contrary to how we often think, we do not have our sin, but our sin has us. We are ruled by it, and it so easily happens with lust when we are consumed by fleshly desires for sexual gratification. My friends, it must not be so. Whatever it may be that leads us to lust must be removed and cast away. It is our very souls that Christ is concerned with here, and we do well to heed his call. We must be certain that we take a vigilant stance against sin. We must be like Job who said, "I have made a covenant with my eyes; how then could I gaze at a virgin?" (Job 31:1)

This is the stance we must embrace as well. One in which we determine before the moment of temptation that we are not going to gaze at others lustfully. Though we may fall short at times, being aware of our inclination to look lustfully at others is key to fighting this particular sin. Because, when we are aware of our potential pitfalls, we can seek ways to avoid them. We can take what is causing temptation and cast it aside in our pursuit to follow the Master of the Sermon.

In what ways may you work to avoid potential pitfalls to lust? Is there a pitfall you are falling into again and again? If so, how might you avoid it altogether?

Day 31: "It was also said, 'Whoever divorces his wife, let him give her a certificate of divorce.'" (5:31)

FOR THE THIRD TIME in the Sermon, we see Jesus correct inadequate teaching. First, he dealt with murder and anger. Then, lust and adultery. Now he deals with a faulty approach to marriage and divorce. Here, Christ begins to call for more than what was permissible under Jewish law, correcting what we may call a low view of marriage. By this I mean a view of marriage in which one party can opt out for whatever reason he or she finds. Perhaps, so they can pursue their own interests or career, find someone else, or avoid marital problems. Or, perhaps, to seek other things they believe will provide them with more happiness. Sound familiar? How many marriages today are dissolved simply because couples are unwilling to work through such issues? So, many take the easier route. They file for divorce and hope for the best in the next stage of life.

Now, I am not advocating for people to stay in abusive or harmful relationships. The Bible has often been misused to lock people into relationships that are harmful to one spouse or the other, and we should fully reject such uses of Scripture. However, I am calling for couples to honor and uphold their marriage vows wherever possible. This means a robust commitment to one another. It means a willingness to do everything in your power to seek reconciliation and to find ways to work through problems so that the marriage can function healthily.

Rather than taking the convenient option, as many modern marriages often do, Jesus is once again calling us to more. He is calling us to think seriously about the vows we make at the altar, requiring us to uphold what we have vowed to uphold. Marriage is difficult, and there will be days when you must wake up and fight for your marriage to survive. It is a covenant that demands patience and humility. However, if you learn the subtle art and skill of sacrifice and submission, you will win the fight for your marriage every single time. You must be consistently pursuing God to do this; and with a mutual commitment to Christ and each other, a marriage can withstand the storms of life.

What is your view on marriage? Is it high or low? Is marriage supposed to only be convenient and easy? Or, has Christ called us to more in our marriages?

Day 32: "But I say to you that everyone who divorces his wife, except on the ground of sexual immorality, makes her commit adultery, and whoever marries a divorced woman commits adultery." (5:32)

THIS VERSE TELLS US how seriously Jesus takes marriage. The logic may not make immediate sense to us, but the deeper we investigate what Jesus is saying the more clearly we can see what the Master is teaching about marriage. First, there is the concession that one spouse may divorce another for marital infidelity. Though, it is not commanded, which leaves open the option for forgiveness and restitution. Second, if sexual immorality is the only concession made for divorce here, it teaches us something significant about sex. It tells us that sexual intimacy between two people is vastly important and it is what unites two individuals to one another—so much so, that defilement of the sexual union is the only concession Jesus allows here for divorce.

This is why Jesus calls it adultery to marry a divorced person. It's because the previous marriage has not been dissolved unless sexual immorality has occurred. So, when a couple divorces simply for lack of happiness, for convenience, or to pursue other interests, they have not truly separated themselves from each other in Jesus' eyes. We may be tempted to think this is unfair. But again, Jesus is pointing us towards a tremendously high view of marriage and of sex. Sex is not some random act between two individuals, but a unique moment of intimacy that bonds one person to another. According to Jesus, sex is such a powerful force between two individuals that it possesses the power to create something new, a marriage. When a man and a woman are joined in a sexual union, they become something completely new with one another.

How then must we consider our own marriages and sexual intimacy? With what importance and honor must we consider sex and marriage? It is crucial that our marriages be united, for it is not simply our own marriages that are at stake. As we saw earlier, it is the proclamation of the gospel itself that is also at stake (Eph 5:31-32). When our marriages are broken, they proclaim a fractured gospel. They profess a gospel in which Christ is content to be estranged from his bride, the Church. However, we know this is not the good news of the gospel. Therefore, let us be lovingly committed to our spouses in every way.

How does Christ's relationship with the Church change our view of marriage? If Christ is not content to be severed from his Church, why would we be content to cut ourselves off from our husbands or wives?

Day 33: "Again you have heard that it was said to those of old, 'You shall not swear falsely, but shall perform to the Lord what you have sworn.'" (5:33)

JUST AS JESUS DESIRES for our marriages to be whole, so does he desire for our speech to be whole. There is no room for double-speak or hypocritical language. Instead, the Master calls us to be uniform in the words we say. We currently live in a world where the weight of our words has decreased significantly. We are unbound to the things we say. Truth has become something that is seemingly up for grabs, and even our most crucial promises (like the vows we take in marriage) are trivialized and can be taken back. We have come to a point where it is quite easy to make bold statements, vows, and promises, and then back out of them with few repercussions. We have come to a place where our words mean very little.

So, what must we do? If words have become so empty and meaningless, how do we reclaim them? We must heed the advice of the Master, particularly noting what he tells us in the upcoming verses: that our speech must be true in every aspect, or it loses its meaning altogether. Again, the Master is calling us to a much higher standard than we would choose for ourselves. Friend, this may seem harsh, but this is part and parcel to what it means to follow Christ as his disciple. It means that we are joyfully obedient to Christ, submitting ourselves to his teachings so that we might be salt and light in this world. And, by doing so, that we may lead others to glorify our Father in heaven.

When our speech is whole and pure, we stand out in a world where words have become cheap and meaningless. We stand out in a world where speaking truthfully is always in question and suspect. So much of the news, media, and even conversation among friends and peers, has been reduced in value. However, when we stand by our words and honor what proceeds from our mouths, we live in such a way that honors the God of truth: "God is not man, that he should lie, or a son of man, that he should change his mind. Has he said, and will he not do it? Or has he spoken, and will he not fulfill it?" (Num 23:19)

In what ways is your speech impure or untrue? How might wholeness in your speech affect your relationships with others? With God?

Day 34: "But I say to you, Do not take an oath at all, either by heaven, for it is the throne of God. . ." (5:34)

OUR WORDS ARE MEANT to be true regardless of the context in which we speak them. It may seem that Jesus is saying to never make promises or vows, but this would be to overgeneralize Jesus' statement. He is teaching us that our "Yes" should mean yes, and our "No" should mean no (Matt 5:37). The Master is telling us that what we say shouldn't have varying levels of truth if we speak in one circumstance or another. Jesus is telling us that what we say at any moment, or in any situation, must be true.

We do not take oaths by heaven because when we speak in any situation, we are to honor the words that proceed from our lips. Truthfulness in speech is required consistently, not just in particular moments where we might be asked to make a vow. We often hear the phrase, "I swear to God . . . ," and by this, people seem to imply that they are most certainly telling the truth. However, the follower of Christ has no need to make such a statement. The reason is that others should know that we will uphold what we say in any situation, whether we have sworn on something or not. When we live by our word daily, there is no need to defend the truthfulness of our speech, as our actions are routinely in line with what we say. Our previous behavior is a testament to our present speech. Therefore, a higher authority is not necessary to defend our words.

This also extends beyond the promises we make. It includes not only what we say, but also how we say it. What I mean is that our very tone, delivery, and phrasing can be just as deceptive as the words we say. There's more than one way to tell a lie. We can easily say something truthful in content but deliver it in such a way so as to deceive the one to whom we speak. Christian, this must not be our way of speaking. Instead, let us be fully whole and truthful in all the things we say and in all the ways that we speak, always fulfilling the promises we make.

In what ways is your speech not fully truthful? Does this apply to your emails and texts? Is your presentation of yourself true on social media or on your resumé?

34

Day 35: ". . .or by the earth, for it is his footstool, or by Jerusalem, for it is the city of the great King." (5:35)

EVEN THE PLACE WHERE God rests his feet is not a thing by which we should swear. This is because the earth, in this verse, finds its significance in that it relates to God. Because of this, it is something by which trifling promises should not be made. In ancient Judaism, Jerusalem was the center of faith and practice. It was the city that held the temple, the place where God resided among his people. It is where God's feet reached down from heaven and touched the earth, so to speak. It was a particular place that held extremely significant value.

Just as we often hear or say, "I swear to God . . . ," we may just as easily swear on things that are central to our faith. For example, in our court system, we place our hands on the Bible and swear to tell the truth. Do I think a Christian shouldn't do this? Some have taken this position, but I don't necessarily think we must. Here, Jesus' teaching is deconstructing the notion that what we might say when swearing on the Bible (or Jerusalem) would be any truer than what we say in any other part of our lives. Just as we would speak truthfully in a court of law, so should we speak truthfully when we are at home or among friends. When we talk to the grocery store clerk, we are called to uphold the same manner of truthfulness that we would before a judge.

Some may refuse to swear on the Bible in court (which you can do), based on the principle that what one says is assuredly true. Or, on the other hand, one may swear simply because it really isn't swearing at all, because the Christian is already committed to speaking truthfully. Either way, the point remains that we as Christians are called to uphold the highest standard of speech in any situation we may find ourselves. At the bank, school, work, the grocery store, online, or even in court, let our speech be whole and consistent in all places and in all ways.

Do you struggle to speak truthfully in all environments? Do you feel that there are some places where you must speak more truthfully than in others? What are they and why?

Day 36: "And do not take an oath by your head, for you cannot make one hair white or black." (5:36)

ARE WE STARTING TO get the point yet? We do not swear by God, heaven, Jerusalem, or even by our own heads. Why? Because our speech should be true no matter what, whether we have sworn a vow or not. The point Jesus is making is that we should not make oaths based on the highest of authorities, God, or even the lowest, our heads, nor anything in between. When we try to make oaths on any of these things, we will inevitably do one of two things.

First, we will trivialize everything we say that does not come with an oath to back up our words. Thus, our words can only be deemed true if we swear by something beyond ourselves. So, we are making a double standard for true speech when some of our words come with oaths and some do not. Or second, we will make every promise with an oath and end up with the same results. If all our speech comes with an oath, the oath no longer means anything either. Either way of using oaths undermines the integrity of our speech.

Instead, our speech must be wholly and completely uniform, free from falsity in every way. The call that the Master of the Sermon makes of us is to speak truthfully in all we say. Now, this is an incredibly difficult task, and it is one that we should not take lightly. In the letter of James, great attention is put forth to describe how difficult it is to truly tame the tongue: "For every kind of beast and bird, of reptile and sea creature, can be tamed and has been tamed by mankind, but no human being can tame the tongue. It is a restless evil, full of deadly poison" (Jas 3:7-8).

Now, perhaps this call seems too high, or even unattainable. However, the call of Jesus remains the same: to speak honestly and truthfully, seeking to continually grow in our discipline of taming the tongue. We do this through the process of sanctification, as we are daily formed into the image of Christ and are better able to live by his commands. Brother and sisters, the call is difficult, but to truly follow Christ means we will make every effort to live and speak as God desires of us.

In what ways do you currently control your tongue? In what ways do you need to continue learning to control your tongue?

Day 37: "Let what you say be simply 'Yes' or 'No';
anything more than this comes from evil." (5:37)

ALL THAT JESUS HAS been speaking about concerning oaths boils down to this one statement. It's actually rather straightforward, isn't it? Yet, we tend to complicate it by trying to figure out how we are going to respond in a given situation or circumstance. We wrestle with what information to disclose and how to disclose it, or what to say and when to say it. All the while, Jesus calls for the basis of speech to be nothing other than speaking truthfully. Letting our "Yes" mean yes, and our "No" mean no.

In light of this, Jesus' teaching on truthfulness in speech must be built into our everyday lives. We should have this manner of speech always in mind so that when we come across any situation, we already know how we are going to respond: with the truth. If we try to decide in the moment, we allow the opportunity for temptation to steer us away from speaking honestly. Instead, we must be committed to speaking truthfully before any such circumstance arrives.

Now, this raises the question, "Does this mean every circumstance?" The classic scenario put forward regarding truthful speech is whether one tells the Nazi officer the truth if you are hiding Jews. This is obviously a much bigger question than what Jesus seeks to address in the Sermon, as well as the type of circumstance in which almost none of us would ever find ourselves. But, in this scenario, one might also consider what larger truths would God have us affirm. For instance, our God is a God of life who seeks the preservation of life, which is a truth we must uphold as well.

Regardless, in the Sermon, Jesus is speaking much more about our day-to-day life rather than every ethical dilemma possible. He speaks of the ordinary situations where it is so tempting and easy to bend or alter the truth for our own benefit. In these situations, the unequivocal answer is the same: to be honest in our speech. We must be truthful and honest in every facet of life and have harmony in our spoken words, our external deeds, and our internal thoughts. It is when we seek to find exceptions to the rule that we inevitably end up defying it.

What are the ordinary situations that are tempting for you to be less honest? What might Jesus mean by saying that false and untrue speech comes from evil?

Day 38: "You have heard that it was said, 'An eye for an eye and a tooth for a tooth.'" (5:38)

THIS VERSE SUMMARIZES THE classic law of retaliation from the Old Testament (Exod 21:23-24; Lev 24:19-20; Deut 19:21). If you harm me, then you are liable to make restitution in an equal manner. If you damage my property, you make an equal payment to restore or replace the damaged property. Simple, right? Well, not quite. As is consistent throughout the Sermon, Jesus is calling us to more than such simplistic readings of the law. We cannot just read it on the surface-level and then move forward. This is exactly what Jesus is teaching against.

The law of retaliation was intended to prevent exorbitant lawsuits in which one party is forced to make payment beyond what was due. It was intended to maintain equality for the inevitable damages that come up in life. However, Jesus is calling us to more than this. As we'll see over the next few days, this is a call for mercy. It is a call to mature and move beyond making sure we always get what we are due and, instead, embrace a posture of forgiveness. It is a call to look past wrongdoing and see the humanity in others, rather than evaluating every situation in monetary terms. When we apply the law from a surface-level reading, our day-to-day circumstances become transactional, ensuring that gain and loss are appropriately meted out between individuals. We lose the human connection to those with whom we interact, as they become the means to our financial ends.

Rather, when we invite the Master's teaching into our lives, our day-to-day circumstances become first and foremost about the person with whom we are interacting. It's no longer about ensuring that we get what we are owed, but that we deal with others compassionately and generously. After all, this is exactly how Christ has dealt with us. If it were about receiving fair retribution, then we would be in a desperate and hopeless situation before God. But, since God has chosen to deal with us mercifully, we can do so for others as well. Brothers and sisters, when we do this, we proclaim the very same good news of forgiveness that was proclaimed through Christ's sacrificial death on the cross.

Do you have a mindset bent towards mercy and forgiveness, or one towards fairness? Is there an example in which you were shown mercy for wrongdoing? If so, how did it change the relationship?

Day 39: "But I say to you, Do not resist the one who is evil. But if anyone slaps you on the right cheek, turn to him the other also." (5:39)

IN THIS GIVEN SCENARIO, our natural reaction seems most fair: to retaliate and slap someone in return. Or, perhaps, strike even harder. After all, would this not be justified by the law Jesus has just mentioned? An eye for an eye, a tooth for a tooth? Therefore, a slap for a slap? Wouldn't it be fair to slap the other person and call it even? Of course, we know what would happen here. We would then be trading slap for slap, gradually increasing the degree of force until an all-out brawl ensued. That is, unless, we were willing to suffer violence and not return it. After all, Christ gave us the perfect example of this on the cross.

This doesn't necessarily mean that we make no defense of ourselves if our lives are at stake. But, at the very least, it means that we refuse to let physical force be our primary means of dealing with problems. Furthermore, though this verse mentions a physical act of violence, the same truth holds for violence in speech. It may not be a slap across the face, but an insult directed toward us. Either way, the principle remains the same. To heed the call of the Master and to not return injustice with further injustice. Instead, the prevailing standard we have before us is to be forgiving and merciful people.

If we suffer wrong in this life, we must be willing to move past it while suffering the brunt of malicious deeds and speech against us. Though every inclination in ourselves would urge us to retaliate, we instead respond to the higher calling of Christ. We seek to be merciful people, peacemakers, those who are persecuted for righteousness sake. It, like so much of the Sermon, is a higher calling that harkens back to the beatitudes that began the Sermon. And, just as the beatitudes are perfectly fulfilled in Christ, so is this verse too: "When he was reviled, he did not revile in return; when he suffered, he did not threaten, but continued entrusting himself to him who judges justly" (1 Pet 2:23). With Christ as our example, let us do the same.

Is your first reaction to wrongdoing to seek revenge, or to forgive?
Is there anyone to whom you could show mercy for wrongdoing?
Would you be willing to do so with Christ as your example?

Day 40: "And if anyone would sue you and take your tunic, let him have your cloak as well." (5:40)

WHETHER WE SUFFER FROM personal injury, insult, or legal action taken against us, we are called to be merciful and forgiving people. Here, we may wish that Jesus could just make it easier for everyone. But he persistently calls us to more, setting the bar high for those who would come and follow him. If we imagine what this statement would even look like, it's even more shocking. If someone were being sued for their tunic, it means that they have nothing else for which they could be sued. The tunic was the inner garment of clothing, underneath the cloak, and the verse implies that this person has no other property for which he or she could be sued. They have no money, no property, no livestock, no personal possessions, but only the clothing on their back.

Here the Master tells us, should we find ourselves in the same position, we should not resist. In case you missed it, this would mean that you are left completely naked. See how high the call it is to be a peacemaker? It goes all the way to the point that we are left completely forsaken of all that we own. It is the call to become like Jesus. Though he was King of the universe and deserving of the most royal clothing, he became nothing for our sake and died on a cross. Forsaken. Alone. Naked.

Here the weight of Jesus' words come fully to bear. We must deny everything possible for the sake of following Christ. We must be willing to part with all material wealth so that we can cling only to Christ and allow him to reign supreme in our hearts. This, my friends, is what makes living a life of abandonment possible. Because, when we truly have Christ, we have all that we could ever need. We may be poor and naked in this life, but we inherit the Kingdom of God and are clothed in Christ's righteousness. Having this perspective is what allows us to be willing to let go of all the things in this life that compete for our allegiance to Christ. My friend, be willing to let go of it all and to have Christ and his kingdom instead.

Is Christ enough for you to abandon everything in this life? When others seek to do you harm, are you willing to be content, given that you have Christ and his kingdom in place of whatever you may lose?

Day 41: "And if anyone forces you to go one mile,
go with him two miles." (5:41)

AT FIRST, THIS STATEMENT may seem somewhat peculiar. Who would force someone to travel a mile? Why would someone be needed to travel a mile? And why would someone oblige this request at all? The context in which Jesus is speaking helps shed some light on this odd request, however. At this time, Israel was under Roman rule, and soldiers would often be traveling around the country. To ease their burden, soldiers would compel citizens of the host country to carry food, supplies, and equipment for them. Jesus says when we find ourselves in this situation, to go two miles instead of the one forced upon us.

This is not because we like to have our time wasted or that we agree with the authority of the Roman government. Nor is it because we are pushovers willing to have our rights infringed upon. Not at all! The reason is that we are embracing a different way of being in this world. We are embodying the life of Christ and his kingdom. We are declaring to an unjust world what mercy and grace look like and that we are willing to show grace and mercy to those who would not do the same in return. We are proclaiming the good news through our willingness to comply with authorities who may not have our best interests in mind.

My brothers and sisters, this is what salt and light look like in a world that is dark and bland. Our actions stand out! Though our inclination may be to revolt and to resist the powers that be, our message is so much clearer when we are gracious to those who are ungracious to us. After all, is this not what Christ did? When asked to bear the cross to Calvary, he did not grumble. He did not seek to enact a coup and rebel against the government, nor did he start a political insurrection. Yet, through his gracious and merciful walk to death, he began to upend the kingdoms of this world and their systems of oppression, and the cross became a symbol of victory, not defeat. Christian, it is by the gracious and merciful pursuit of Christ's kingdom that we do the same in our own lives, walking in the footsteps of the one who carried a Roman instrument of death to the full measure that was required.

Is your inclination to resist people and institutions of authority? How might Christ's example change our stance on how we relate to those who do not have our welfare in mind?

Day 42: "Give to the one who begs from you, and do not refuse the one who would borrow from you." (5:42)

THIS VERSE CONCLUDES THE section of the Sermon that began with the phrase, "An eye for an eye and a tooth for a tooth" (Matt 5:38). The command to not seek retaliation seems to be working backward for Jesus. Not only do we not retaliate when we are wronged, but we instead strive to give charitably. We are not only gracious to those who may offend us, but we are also gracious to those whom we may not necessarily have a reason to be gracious toward.

We all know who falls into this category. I'm quite certain that everyone reading this has passed by "that person" on the street who is asking for some spare change. Or, we may have "that family member" who is always in need of some financial assistance. Jesus says to give generously to this person. Of course, we may protest and say that we are enabling that person, or that we aren't really improving their situation since we are only making them more dependent on others. However, Jesus doesn't seem so concerned about such arguments. He simply says to give to the one that begs. He doesn't say how much or how regularly you are to give, but there is the expectation from the Master that those who follow him will have a spirit of generosity in which they are willing to aid the needs of those who cannot provide for themselves.

When we think of the spiritual poverty we all have before God, while remembering the great cost God paid freely with his only Son, perhaps we ought to be a little more cheerful when someone asks us to spare a dollar. We should also realize that anything we do possess is a gift from God himself and, therefore, we are only temporary owners of the things God has given us anyway. If so, shouldn't we be more willing to part with what we have, rather than clinging to it tightly and shouting, "Mine!" My friend, we must follow the Master here who, though he possessed all of creation, was willing to lay it all down so that you and I may be redeemed. If this cannot teach us selflessness, then nothing will.

Do you have a posture of generosity towards the needy? What prevents you from giving freely? What will you lose if you do so? What might you gain?

Day 43: "You have heard that it was said, 'You shall love your neighbor and hate your enemy.'" (5:43)

Our natural inclination as human beings is to love those who love us and to hate those who hate us. Whoever is on our side we call an ally, but whoever is not is our enemy. However, the kingdom that Christ speaks of in the Sermon allows for no such thinking. In this portion of the Sermon, Christ will challenge the notion that we naturally have, which is to despise those who are our enemies.

Is this not the root of so much strife, envy, and hate in this world? Nations hate other nations because of cultural, religious, political, and ethnic differences. People hate others because of envy, greed, jealousy, and pride. Hate breeds more hate as we seek to retaliate against the hate directed toward us, creating a vicious cycle of enmity between people and communities that only ends in the destruction of others. So much of this hate stems from petty differences and ignorance of the "other," the one who is not exactly like us. We don't seek to understand those we think are against us; we automatically assume that they are evil and, therefore, our hate towards them is justified.

My friend, we cannot follow Christ and think this way; it is simply unallowable and inconsistent with Christ's call upon our lives. We must remember that, as sinners once estranged from God, we were enemies of the Lord, committing treason against the true King as we sought to live as lords over our own lives. But, we have hope through Christ, as Paul told the church in Rome: "God shows his love for us in that while we were still sinners, Christ died for us" (Rom 5:8) Christian, this is how God came to you while you were still his enemy. If that is the case, how much more should we seek to love our enemies instead of hating them?

How does Christ's love towards his enemies change the way we view our enemies? How can love change our relationship to those who are our enemies?

Day 44: "But I say to you, Love your enemies and pray for those who persecute you. . ." (5:44)

THE DISCIPLE OF CHRIST is someone who operates from a posture and position of love, showing grace and mercy to those who may be our enemies. Those who follow the path of Christ are individuals who extend love to all, show love to the foreigner, the outsider, those on the periphery of society, and the social pariahs. Not only these, but also our physical enemies and those who may purposefully seek to harm us: those who hate us for one reason or another and are willing to take up arms to bring us harm.

In June of 2015, a man entered a historically black church in Charleston, South Carolina, and sat among those gathered for Bible study. Within a few moments, he pulled out a gun and opened fire upon them, killing nine people and injuring others. It is tragic to see that hate and racism are still such prevalent and catastrophic factors in our society. However, it is the response of this church and the victims' family members that is so amazing and worth remembering amid this tragedy. Facing the shooter in person, the people of Emanuel African Methodist Episcopal Church forgave their enemy. Family members of those who lost their lives stood face-to-face with the shooter and, one after another, forgave the man who murdered their loved ones.

This, my brothers and sisters, is what it looks like to live out Jesus' teaching here in the Sermon. This is what it is to love our enemies and pray for those who persecute us. Though we have heard it said through conventional wisdom that we should hate those who would harm us, we are instead called to love unconditionally and in a radical way. This radical way of love is such that it extends to those who hate us and seek our demise. But, if we are to follow Christ's path as the people of Emanuel Church did, then we must be ever ready to love, pray for, and forgive those who hate us.

How does loving our enemies bear witness to the world around us? Who are enemies in your life that you are called to love? Are you loving them?

44

Day 45: ". . .so that you may be sons of your Father who is in heaven. For he makes his sun rise on the evil and on the good, and sends rain on the just and on the unjust." (5:45)

IF THERE IS ANY question remaining for whether we should love our enemies, this verse should immediately expel it. This verse tells us that our identity as children of God is what is at stake regarding how we treat our enemies. If we do not love our enemies, then we are not children of God. However, if we do, then we bear the mark as true followers of Christ and children of the Father. We may not like this notion or feel that it is too harsh. But, as we are reminded, God loved us even while we were his enemies and, therefore, we are to do the same.

Not for this reason alone, but also because so many of God's blessings, such as the sun's warmth and light and the rain's nourishment to the earth, are given freely to all. God does not withhold sun and rain from the evil and give it only to the good, but abundantly provides for all of creation out of his common grace. The Christian's love must be the same, going forth to all and not reserved only for those who love us. When we love only those who love us in return, we practice a selfish type of love. A type of love in which there is no risk of rejection or hurt, but a type that is only based upon reciprocity rather than serving others in joy.

Friend, we are called to love sacrificially, giving ourselves as Christ gave himself. We are called to love freely, not expecting things in return that make the balance even and compensate for the things we have done. We are called to love even when it may cost us, knowing that this is our duty. It means loving even if those who receive our love will refuse it or waste it, leaving us empty, alone, and with nothing to show for our efforts. This is, in fact, exactly what Christ's love towards us looked like before we knew him, and this is what it looks like for so many who still refuse him. In light of this, my friend, love others graciously and with self-abandonment, knowing that Jesus has done the very same for you.

Who are you tempted to not love well? Do you truly believe that the cost of loving those who do not love you in return is worth it? Why or why not?

Day 46: "For if you love those who love you, what reward do you have? Do not even the tax collectors do the same?" (5:46)

FIRST, JESUS IS NOT telling us that we should not love those who love us in return. Naturally, we love those who love us, and we don't need a reminder to do so since our most natural instincts compel us in this regard. It is those who are our enemies that we must be reminded to love; those whom we would prefer not to love at all. Or, those individuals for whom we would find any reason to justify our hatred toward. But it is these very people who we are to love if we are to pursue the kingdom and call ourselves disciples of Christ.

This is the type of love that stands out in the world, like salt or light. People will naturally love those who are like them, who run in similar social circles, or who are a part of the same community. But, when our love reaches beyond those boundaries, it truly becomes a witness to the rest of the world. It means our love must cross over to nations who may despise us, people groups who might subject us, or those in authority who do not have our welfare in mind. This, my friend, is a powerful type of love. It is not the quaint love that exists between two similar people, but it is a fierce and covenantal love that bears witness to Christ's radical love towards us. Just as Christ's love traversed the infinite gap between a holy God and a sinful world, so should our love bridge the smaller gaps that exist between ourselves and others.

When we love in this way, steadfastly and fiercely, our love can transform the world around us. It's the type of love that causes others to take notice, and it's the type of love that can transform lost and wayward hearts and point them towards God. Christian, this is what the love of Christ must look like in our lives. It must seek those who may utterly reject us, despise us, and downright hate us, and then love them steadfastly and compassionately in return, echoing the gospel of love that Christ has shown us in his life.

How does Christ offer us a bigger picture of love towards others?
Why is loving our enemies so important to our witness to Christ?

Day 47: "And if you greet only your brothers, what more are you doing than others? Do not even the Gentiles do the same?" (5:47)

JUST AS WE LOVE our enemies, so should we greet and show hospitality to those who are not our brothers and sisters or a part of our community. Here, the commandment to love is to be expressed even in our most common and everyday interactions. We are called, as Christians, to extend greetings to others, show hospitality, pay respect, and to joyfully welcome others as they are. Again, this displays the radical love of Christ and bears testimony to the Lord, but it is also a deeply humanizing act. It means that we recognize the intrinsic worth of all of humanity and honor the image of God within others.

When we do this, it becomes quite difficult to hate others. When we do this, it's hard to see others as "sub-human" or inferior to ourselves. It also gives us an honest image of ourselves, as we see the same image of God within ourselves in other people. We cannot do this and then lie about others, slander them, mistreat them, abuse them, devalue them, manipulate them, hurt them, kill them, or anything else. To do so would be to deny the image of God they bear, as well the image of God we bear. To do these things is to state that the value with which God has endowed humanity is insignificant and meaningless. Or worse, to state that others do not bear the image of God at all and, therefore, are less than human.

My friend, this is something we cannot do as followers and disciples of Christ. When all these things are left behind, the only thing left for us to do is to approach others with grace and value them for the worth they carry as people loved and providentially cared for by God. This defies our modern notions of class and our valuing of others by their wealth, beauty, or intelligence. My friend, you and every other person in this world are valuable by virtue of being created to bear the image of God. Therefore, let us love and greet one another, showing hospitality and giving testimony to the Lord of all creation who graces us by creating us in his image.

Are you tempted to assume people are lesser, inferior, or lacking in importance? Which people do you need to acknowledge the image of God within that you currently do not?

Day 48: "You therefore must be perfect, as
your heavenly Father is perfect." (5:48)

THIS VERSE CONCLUDES THE first major section of the Sermon containing Christ's teaching on what it is to truly fulfill the law, and it does so in a grand fashion. Perfection? What an unattainable goal! Furthermore, could not this idea of "perfection" lead to diminished views of ourselves and cause despair? Especially in a world dominated by social media platforms flaunting those with "perfect" lives, families, and bodies? Besides that, doesn't Scripture itself teach us quite the opposite, that we are broken and sinful people in need of redemption? Surely it does. But Scripture also teaches us of God's holiness and desire for humanity to be holy.

Before we lose hope, let's consider a few things. First, the word "perfect" in this verse could also be translated as "whole" or "complete." The idea is that we must be fully who God has created us to be. This means that we are consistent inwardly and outwardly in our lives, speech, thought, and actions. It means our whole self is in unison and working to live as God has designed us. Second, we must also remember that this is a process called sanctification, and it is slow work. We do not suddenly have it all together when we begin to follow Christ, or even after we have followed him 50 years. Think of the disciples who originally heard Christ's words spoken. Following this moment, they would make numerous mistakes that would fall short of their call. However, the overall trajectory of their lives was to become more Christlike. There were ups and downs along the way, but they gradually followed Christ more closely each day.

Finally, we must remember that Christ himself lived the perfect life. He lived a life that satisfied the perfection his Father in heaven desires. And, it is through Christ's works that we are saved, not our own. Christ fulfilled the Sermon in every aspect of his life, then died on behalf of every one of us who will fail to do so. Because of this, God looks upon us and sees Christ's righteousness. So, we do not abandon the teachings of the Sermon because they are too hard. Instead, we are reminded that the Sermon has been fulfilled in Christ and that God will continue to sanctify us through Christ and fulfill God's Word in us as we come into Christ's kingdom.

Do you ever feel that you have to be perfect? Do you feel that others seem to be "perfect," or have it all together? How does Christ's perfection change how we view ourselves?

Day 49: "Beware of practicing your righteousness before other people in order to be seen by them, for then you will have no reward from your Father who is in heaven." (6:1)

THE FIRST VERSE OF chapter 6 provides an opening statement introducing what Jesus will be speaking about through the first half of the chapter (Matt 6:1-18). You might call it "hidden righteousness." This is partially true but, primarily, Jesus is speaking against false outward righteousness, which isn't righteousness at all. Here, the idea of legalism falls completely flat on its face in the Sermon.

Where legalism preaches external actions on display for all to see, Christ instead teaches that such things earn us no reward from our Father who is in heaven. Where legalism affirms earning our salvation through deeds, Christ says deeds done for outward show are worthless, earning us nothing but trivial praise in this life. Where legalism espouses devotion to religiosity devoid of faith and repentance, Christ instead preaches devotion to God through obedience. This is not to say that our external actions are of no importance, however. Instead, it is to say that our inward piety and desire to please God should come first. Then, from this place of internal devotion, our outward actions flow and do so from our commitment to serve and honor God, rather than trying to bring honor to ourselves.

John the Baptist provides us a perfect example, "[Jesus] must increase, but I must decrease" (John 3:30). Unfortunately, these words are the antithesis of our modern world and way of thinking. We are chronically ill with the notion that we are most important, deserving of the most praise, and should have the most influence. We have Stage IV cancer when it comes to pride, plaguing every aspect of our lives, and attaching itself to everything we do. Whether it is to earn the most money, have the most followers, seem the happiest, fittest, or most intelligent, every aspect of what we do has become an attempt of reorienting the universe toward ourselves. This, Christian friends, is where we need emergency surgery. We need Christ to use his scalpel and cut away the sickness that poisons our lives and relationship with God. We need the great Healer to do a dramatic work in us so that we may begin to truly live to God's glory, and not our own.

In what ways do you practice your righteousness as a show for others? What will it look like for you to repent of this?

Day 50: "Thus, when you give to the needy, sound no trumpet before you, as the hypocrites do in the synagogues and in the streets, that they may be praised by others. Truly, I say to you, they have received their reward." (6:2)

IT IS SO EASY for us to pollute good deeds with false motivations. Often, we are like the hypocrites whom Jesus addresses here, doing good deeds but from a place of pride. We so easily do the good works God has called us to for self-motivated purposes, hoping that such acts may curry favor with our peers or with God. But, shouldn't we receive recognition for the good things we do for those who are in need? Shouldn't we be affirmed for our selflessness and care for others? Notice that Jesus does not condemn the hypocrites in this verse for *receiving* recognition, but for *seeking* it.

That is the big difference! They have made a show of themselves and their giving, placing their egos in the spotlight so that everyone may witness their "generosity." In contrast, we may do good deeds and we may receive recognition for them, but recognition should never be our motivation for doing good deeds in the first place. That is the problem Jesus is addressing, those who do good works solely to receive others' praise. It is not the act of giving to the poor, it is not that people see that the poor are being cared for, but it is giving in such a way as to be seen.

Jesus, as he does consistently throughout the Sermon, is going to the heart of the matter. Legalism would suggest that as long as you care for the needy, you may prove yourself righteous. Jesus says that how you care for the needy is just as important. It cannot be done to increase one's own status or image but must be done from a humble heart seeking to receive the rewards of heaven, rather than the praise of man. When we give in this way, we redirect all the praise from ourselves to God and can serve those in need rather than serving ourselves. Doing so, we truly care about the poor and their needs, rather than caring just about how we are seen by others.

When are you tempted to do good deeds before others or for show? How does this rob God of his glory? What might humble generosity look like in your life?

Day 51: "But when you give to the needy, do not let your left hand know what your right hand is doing. . ." (6:3)

IN OUR LIVES, THE discipline of giving must be such that those who may know us best are unaware. Jesus' metaphor in this verse suggests that the way we give must be one-sided. That means it cannot be for the act of giving and for showing off the deed at the same time. In our modern world where cash is handled less and less, this may not make quite as much sense. But if we think of this metaphor in the times of Jesus, when money and wealth existed only in physical forms, it makes much more sense.

In those times, to help the poor one would have to physically hand money to the one in need. Jesus is saying that when you do this, the act should be so discreet that even the hand on the other side of your body is unaware. In our modern age, it is in some ways easier to do this, but in other ways harder. It is easier in the fact that we can make an online donation or write a check without showing off to those around us how much or when we give. We can set up recurring donations or text in a contribution with no one being the wiser. However, it's harder in that we can easily hit the "share" button to social media and alert the world of our "generosity," ensuring that our friends and family are aware of how much we care for those in need. Even if our methods for giving in the modern world can more easily be anonymous to those around us, the temptation to boast and make our "charitable giving" known to others remains the same.

It is also harder in that we can easily use this verse to hide our lack of giving as well. When asked if we help the poor, we can conceal our lack of care and concern by hiding behind this verse, suggesting that our giving is done in secret and unseen and therefore is not obvious to others. When we do this, we not only lack compassion for the poor that the Sermon requires of us, but we also lie and use Scripture to do so. Instead, we must do what the Sermon teaches. The verses here call us to be compassionate, but not with the sort of false compassion that seeks our own praise. Instead, we must have the type of compassion that seeks to glorify God through our deeds and seeks his approval, not the world's.

Is there an appropriate balance between giving and raising awareness of the needs of others? How might we check our motivations for giving so that we may give with pure intentions and not selfish desires?

Day 52: ". . .so that your giving may be in secret. And your Father who sees in secret will reward you." (6:4)

THE SUMMARIZING POINT IS that our giving must be done modestly. It is not showy. It is not to inflate our own egos. And, it is not so that we may receive the praise of others. It is secret, hidden, and discreet. Though discreet, it does not go unnoticed. In fact, every good deed that we do in private is seen. Our deeds are seen by the audience that truly matters, the Lord himself. It is he who takes notices of our giving that is done discreetly, and the reward that he offers is exceedingly greater than anything we may receive from our peers.

Our peers may reward us with praise, pats on the back, and words of affirmation. Or, we may be remembered as generous and caring, as people who defend the cause of the needy. Yet, all such rewards are fleeting and eventually pass away. They are transient and, ultimately, will be forgotten. However, our Father in heaven wants to give us a much greater reward for our giving. He wants to give us treasures in heaven (Matt 6:19-21)! That is the reward that our hidden righteousness and hidden deeds earn! It is the true riches of the kingdom which God desires to offer us, and it is these same riches that we forsake when our giving is done for show.

Christ draws a line in the sand for us here. It is one or the other when it comes to the rewards we receive for our giving. Either we practice our righteousness for public show and receive public praise, or we practice our righteousness in secret and receive the eternal riches of the kingdom. The choice truly is ours, but we are not without warning. We have heard the teaching of the Master, and we know which route we ought to take. This is never easy, as our pride continually nags at us to seek recognition. However, the way of Christ demands that we practice our giving privately and with humility, seeking to please our Father in heaven rather than our peers.

Does the promise of the Father's rewards help reorient our perspective on giving? What do we stand to gain, and what do we stand to lose if we embrace Christ's desire for how we give?

Day 53: "And when you pray, you must not be like the hypocrites. For they love to stand and pray in the synagogues and at the street corners, that they may be seen by others. Truly, I say to you, they have received their reward." (6:5)

JUST AS OUR GIVING is to be in secret, so is our prayer. The temptation may be to put our reverence, piety, and devotion to God on display, but Jesus tells us to seek our Father in quiet solitude. Now, there is the pitfall to misinterpret this verse just as there is with the rest of the Sermon. Does this mean we never pray publicly? What about at church or at Bible study? Before a meal, in the hospital, and so forth? Of course, we pray in such scenarios, and we should. But, notice, the motivation is again what is askew, not the deed itself.

In this verse, the hypocrites pray publicly, "that they may be seen by others." Their motivation is not to enter into genuine dialogue with the Lord, but to be seen and noticed. It is so their "righteousness" is on display before all others, that they might be seen as holier than thou. My friend, unfortunately, such actions still persist in the church today. We have all seen the person who wants to make sure everyone knows that they really are a devout follower of Jesus. Whether that be how they pray, sing, fellowship, etc. We still see so many who are quite persistent in making sure you know how spiritually elite they are. The problem then becomes discerning what is true character and what is a false show. Furthermore, how are we to truly know the motivations of these individuals?

Well, that is not our role. This verse is not telling us to identify who is practicing their righteousness for show and who is not. It is telling us that we need to evaluate ourselves and our motivations. Jesus is forcing us to ask, "Do I pray this way?" When we ask this diagnostic question of ourselves, we may find that we do not like the answer. We may find that there are a plethora of broken, selfish, and deceitful ambitions that motivate our actions. We can mask it in religiosity, but the call of the Master is to recognize these sinful desires in us and to eradicate them. To do so means stepping out of the limelight where our pride likes to dwell and stepping silently into the hidden and quiet places. It is there that we can truly repent and learn to pray again.

Why and how do you pray? What stimulates you to pray? Is the way you pray in public and private the same, or is there something different in these two locations?

Day 54: "But when you pray, go into your room and shut the door and pray to your Father who is in secret. And your Father who sees in secret will reward you." (6:6)

OFTEN, OUR PRIDEFUL HEARTS need quietness and solitude to relearn humility. Even in spiritual matters, our tendency is to elevate ourselves and make ourselves seem more than who we truly are. However, in the quietness of our rooms, we have no space for being flashy or showy. Our volume, fervor, or eloquence is unheard, and the methods of speech that may impress a crowd are instantly stripped away. Instead, we must come before God alone, where the words we pray are all we have to offer. We come directly before God, who hears the most polished prayers of the faithful and the stumbled over words of the sinner just the same. It is in this space we learn to truly pray to our Father.

When we pray to be seen, our communication is not with God. It is with those whom we hope will witness our act of devotion. Though our words may seem to be directed to the Lord, they are in fact directed towards others, and this reveals whose approval we truly seek. Instead, our private prayers can have only one person for our audience, God himself. It is this type of prayer that God will reward, and the reward is not based upon the content of the prayer. God does not require that our hidden prayers only be praiseworthy and full of thanksgiving, but leaves room for us to come to him with our deepest woes, confessions, and complaints. After all, this is what a majority of the Psalms look like.

If God is comfortable with preserving such desperate pleas as the Psalms in Scripture, then we can safely assume that he is comfortable with them in the privacy of our own homes. It is this type of honest prayer that God desires from us, prayer that truly seeks him first. It is prayer that seeks to commune with God concerning the things that weigh on our hearts. Though our modern world tells us to broadcast and advertise everything about ourselves, our Father only asks that we come to him in solitude and stillness, forsaking the approval of others that we may be known by him.

Do you have a private prayer life or only a public one? How might having a private prayer life enable you to pray more honestly and more truly?

Day 55: "And when you pray, do not heap up empty phrases as the Gentiles do, for they think that they will be heard for their many words." (6:7)

WE HAVE ALL SAT through that church service, or Bible study, or prayer before a meal, wondering how long So-and-So is going to pray. We feel like we're hanging on the edge of eternity as an incessant drone of piled up phrases repeats, over and over, while we ponder if this is what the kingdom is actually like. Fortunately, Christ himself says this is not what kingdom prayer is. Kingdom prayer comes directly to God, knowing the character of God and being assured that he indeed listens to us. We do not need to get God's attention by talking on and on, babbling a plethora of empty words.

Instead, we come to God knowing that he desires to hear our prayers and he hears them as an intimate listener, knowing what lies at the heart of our prayers. God doesn't need to decipher our words and piece them together like we do when we communicate with others. Not at all! He hears our prayers with a father's heart and truly understands what we have to say. So, when we pray, we can be to the point. It does us no good to think and pray in such a way that is simply circular talk, speaking roundabout phrases that avoid the issue at hand. When we pray, we can say something once, not having to repeat it.

Now, this does not mean that we never pray for the same things multiple times and never have lengthy moments of prayer. Rather, it means that we do not have to tediously find every possible way to articulate what we are saying to God in a single prayer, hoping that it will help God hear. He knows our prayers before we even pray them. God desires that we come to him straightforwardly, rather than trying to heap up as many words as we possibly can to get his attention. Christ tells us that our prayers need only to state the facts. They do not need to be filled with long flowing sentences or fancy words; they need simply to lay our hearts before the Lord who listens. Our prayers do not need to be like the Pharisee who sought to justify himself before God (Luke 18:11-12) but can be as succinct as the tax-collector who stood nearby, "God, be merciful to me, a sinner!" (Luke 18:13b)

Are your prayers long and drawn out for impure motivations? Are you able to come to God and be to the point? Are you ever tempted to evaluate how good/bad your spiritual life is based on the length of your prayers?

Day 56: "Do not be like them, for your Father knows what you need before you ask him." (6:8)

IF WE ARE EVER afraid to pray, feel that our lowly concerns should not be brought to God, or that we are too sinful to pray, this verse should expel any doubts we have about coming to God in prayer. Our Father knows what we need even before we begin to utter our prayers. That is how invested the God of the universe is in us. He is not far off and distant, but is nearer to us than our very breath. He is perfectly aware of exactly who we are, knowing our slightest woes to our deepest despairs. He knows our desires, pleas, praise, and every aspect of our joy as well as our suffering. The things we think may be hidden in the deepest recesses of our hearts are laid bare before God like a book for him to read. Moreover, he is the very author of that book.

So, why pray? If God knows everything we might have the audacity to bring before him in prayer, what is the purpose of us saying these prayers at all? Well, one thing we must remember is that prayer not only lays our hearts open before God, but it also does a work in us. It forms and shapes us, realigning our hearts to be in sync with our Creator. Prayer teaches us to seek God constantly with trust, and it teaches us that God's timing may not be our own. Prayer also teaches us that our Father's will may not be the same as ours. Furthermore, when we pray, we give a voice to the pains and praises that are within us. Although God knows these things already, he still desires to hear them from us.

Think of a spouse who never says, "I love you," or audibly speaks out his or her concerns. Even though his or her partner may know their spouse loves them or what they are thinking, they still need to hear these things said. It creates a bond between the two, strengthening the relationship. Prayer works the same way. It draws us closer into the relationship we need most and strengthens the bond we have between ourselves and God. Though God knows the very words we will say when we come to him in prayer, for our own sake and the sake of our spiritual well-being, we still need to say them.

Does God's knowledge of you stimulate or stifle your desire to pray? Why or why not? How might you grow in your prayer life given God's knowledge of who you are?

Day 57: "Pray then like this: "Our Father in heaven, hallowed be your name." (6:9)

WE'VE SAID THE WORDS of this prayer so many times that we fail to remember how powerful of a prayer it truly is. Jesus not only gives us a format for our own prayers, but also provides us with a rich teaching on who God is. We do not only have a way to pray, but also a glimpse of God's character, showing us why we ought to pray to him. He is our Father, meaning that we are his children. We are in a close relationship with our Maker. He is not a distant ruler far removed and estranged from his people. Instead, he is near, caring for the daily needs of his children.

However, though God is near, he is also in heaven. God is near in relationship and care for his people, yet he is fully transcendent in character and holiness. He is heavenly. We must hold on to the balance of God being fully immanent in his relationship with us while acknowledging that he is still wholly other. Relationally, he is nearer to us than the air in our lungs, yet entirely outside of who we are in his character and holiness. Thus, it is appropriate to ascribe holiness to him and to acknowledge his perfect character. And notice that statement, "hallowed be your name." It is not simply an attributive statement; it is declarative.

We're not saying we think God is holy. When we say these words, we are stating the fact that God is indeed holy. It is not true because we say it; it is true and, therefore, we profess it. His name, which represents the entirety of who God is, is perfectly hallowed, holy in every way. He is righteous in his deeds, thoughts, actions, relationships, and anything else we could ever imagine. Brothers and sisters, this is the God who hears our prayers! When we utter our feeble words that seem so inadequate, stumbling over every phrase, or find ourselves blubbering through tears in an incoherent stream of consciousness, the ever-present and holy Father hears every single word we cry.

How does God's character invite you to trust him in prayer? Are you ever tempted to think that God is distant and does not hear or answer your prayers? How does Christ's reliance on the Father in prayer comfort you to pray with faith?

Day 58: "Your kingdom come, your will be done, on earth as it is in heaven." (6:10)

THERE IS BEAUTIFUL COMFORT in this statement. It serves as a reminder that the life we experience here on earth is not the same as God's heavenly kingdom. The Kingdom of God and the kingdom of man are qualitatively different from one another. Otherwise, there would be no need for Jesus to pray for the Father's kingdom to come. The very fact that these words are prayed by Christ tells us that there is a better way of existing on this earth, and these words also tell us that God desires for his kingdom to be brought to earth. After all, it is Christ, who is fully God and man, who is praying this prayer and asking for the Kingdom of Heaven to reign on earth.

Furthermore, this verse of the Lord's Prayer, also suggests that God's will is not always carried out in this life. This can offer us consolation when we are confronted with the woes that we witness in this world. Whether it be war, famine, racism, poverty, or natural disaster, we know that God's will is being worked against by the power of sin and evil in this world. This does not mean God is not sovereign, all-powerful, and benevolent, but that the ramifications of sinfulness are strong forces that seek to thwart the will of God. Ultimately, however, God's will shall come to pass. We pray to this end in the present, knowing that God is bringing about the redemption and reconciliation of all things. All the travails that plague this life will be brought to an end in God's kingdom.

Of course, the pains of this life are still present. Yet, God is still working to redeem the suffering we experience throughout this life. When we see suffering and strife, it may be tempting to despair. However, we can pray confidently to the Lord, knowing that he is working to establish his kingdom on earth despite the forces of sin that work against it. That means, my friend, that we can be filled with hope, assured that the Kingdom of God is on the move and breaking into this world even now.

Do you struggle to believe that the Kingdom of God is at work within this sinful and broken world? How might praying the Lord's Prayer reframe your view of God's sovereign reign that is being established here on earth?

Day 59: "Give us this day our daily bread. . ." (6:11)

SINCE WE HAVE A loving Father, we can come to him with our most basic needs. We do not have to fret and fear about the physical needs we have, but simply come to the Lord in prayer, trusting that he will provide for the things we need. But notice, it is not for the things we desire. It is not for extravagant possessions or the superfluous objects of this world, but it is a prayer for our most basic sustenance. It is simply asking God to provide food for us each day.

In our modern society, we might not even feel the need for this prayer. For many of us, it is typically answered without us even praying these words. Our daily food is given to us with little to no thought on our part and, to be honest, we take the food we have for granted. So, perhaps, for those of us who do not have to pray this prayer as trustfully as many in the world, the words are an invitation to look at what we have from a posture of thankfulness and gratitude. Or, maybe the words of this prayer are ones that we should pray on behalf of those who do not have a daily source of food. Perhaps the words of this verse should force us to ask how we can be the answer to this prayer for others.

Some may scoff at these words because many have prayed these words over and over again, but to no avail. It's easy to ask why God hasn't answered this prayer for the vast populations around the world who lack daily provision. Instead, we should perhaps ask why we are not trying to be the answer to this prayer for others? Why, if we know the needs of our communities and surrounding neighborhoods, do we not graciously offer the blessings we have from God to others? God desires to use his Church to bless the world and proclaim his favor, and we can do so by offering the bread with which we have been blessed. So, the only question that remains is whether we will choose to do so or not.

Are you inclined to take God's blessing of food for granted? How might you embrace a posture of gratitude towards the food you have? How might you be an answer to this prayer for others?

Day 60: ". . .and forgive us our debts, as we also have forgiven our debtors." (6:12)

WE COME TO GOD not only for the physical things we need but also for the daily forgiveness we need. We come, not with the attitude that we have it all together, but as sinners who recognize our spiritual bankruptcy before a holy and perfect God. We come with debt, owing to God something we have not given: a holy and obedient life. When we think of it in terms of debt, we can also see that the debt in our lives is accruing. Furthermore, we come with the full recognition that any good deeds we do fail to serve as a credit to remove the debts we have.

So, we must come to God to have our debt removed because there is no other way. It is only Christ's righteousness that can serve as a credit to our indebted account, and this is a divine transaction that only occurs through God's grace. Though we recognize our sinfulness before the Lord, we should also be reminded that we come to a good and merciful Father who desires to forgive us our debts. What great encouragement this is to the weary soul! Because of this, we can then embrace a posture of forgiveness towards others as well. Did you catch that? The forgiveness we so desperately need from the Father serves as the basis for how we are to interact with others. It is because we have been forgiven so freely that we may adopt an attitude of mercy and grace towards those who wrong us in this life.

When we reflect on the sin in our lives and see that it all has been forgiven and nailed to the cross, shouldn't we much more readily be able to forgive the misdeeds done towards us? This is not to minimize how we have been wronged, nor is it to say that when we are sinned against it doesn't hurt, damage, or even ruin relationships. However, it does mean that we are still willing to forgive. After all, if God in his perfection is willing to forgive all the sinfulness of humanity, shouldn't we as sinners be willing to forgive the sinners in our midst?

Is there anything, right now, that you need to bring before God to receive forgiveness from? Is there forgiveness that you need to extend to someone else right now? How might knowing that God has forgiven all your sins lead you to forgive others?

Day 61: "And lead us not into temptation, but deliver us from evil." (6:13)

OH, HOW MUCH DO we need to pray this verse! So easily we are drawn to the things of this world and all that it offers to tempt and allure us. We are incessantly barraged by things that can draw us away from the one true God, and quite often we give in to the enticing offerings we find before us. Whether that be food, money, sex, pride, power, etc., we are constantly allured by items that soon become idols. Usually, the things we desire aren't necessarily evil in and of themselves. However, once they've become idols, they supplant our Lord who is meant to rule over our lives.

Therefore, we must daily ask God to lead our hearts away from what entices us and will ultimately destroy us. Now, it is important to note, that although God does not tempt us himself (Jas 1:13), it does not mean that he will not allow us to be tempted. God drove Jesus into the wilderness for the very purpose of being tempted (Matt 4:1). Likewise, God may put us in situations where we may be tempted. But, the crucial thing to note here is that God does not put us in situations of temptation to fail, but to succeed. It is to make us stronger, more disciplined, and obedient followers of Christ. Christ desires that we become more sanctified, not by withdrawal from the world and its temptations, but by being able to resist the temptations the world throws our way.

This is how we may be salt and light, or testimony-bearing witnesses, to the transformative power of God. This is how we declare what it looks like to be citizens of God's kingdom. Now, we must always be careful not to fall into the lie of legalism, suggesting that if we simply follow a set of rules, we might justify ourselves. But we should strive to live by God's commands, knowing that his Spirit enables us to follow them and that our justification comes through God's free grace. This, after all, is all the more reason for us to pray these words. We know that, sooner or later, we will inevitably succumb to temptation and need God's grace. Thankfully, God is always merciful to forgive.

In what ways may God be seeking to make you more obedient through temptations in your life? Which temptations come to you that you need to resist? Which temptations do you lead yourself into that you need God to steer you away from?

Day 62: "For if you forgive others their trespasses, your heavenly Father will also forgive you. . ." (6:14)

THE ONLY PART OF the Lord's Prayer that Jesus provides further comment on is regarding forgiveness. Why is this? Perhaps it is because Christ knows that we are quite apt to withhold forgiveness. Afterall, Jesus has already told us that the merciful will receive mercy (Matt 5:7) and that we must be reconciled to others before we come to God in worship (Matt 5:23-24). So, maybe we need extra reminders on this matter? We may think we have forgiven others, but instead, we have chosen to move on without attempting to reconcile the broken relationship.

So, we must be reminded once again that to follow Christ is to actively forgive others. It doesn't start with those who ask for forgiveness, and it is not those who have come to us apologizing for wrongs committed. Nor does it start with those who refuse to admit to any wrongdoing in the first place. Forgiveness begins with disciples of Christ. When an offense occurs, it is we who must bridge the gap between ourselves and others. Christ does not tell us to wait until the other party is truly worthy of forgiveness, but commands that we forgive regardless of the offense or whether or not the offender has shown remorse. It's simple really: You are a forgiven follower of Christ; therefore, you forgive others. Of course, there may still be pain, and the offense may create a rift in the relationship that cannot be repaired. However, the posture of the heart of a true disciple is one that offers forgiveness for trespasses against us.

This kind of forgiveness not only seeks reconciliation, but also allows us to relinquish the burden of unforgiveness. It permits us to bestow the blessing of forgiveness we know so well as Christ's redeemed people. It is an act that proclaims the gospel of grace to others, declaring that sin can be forgiven and reconciliation can occur between those estranged from each other, just as we who were once separated from God are now reconciled to him through God's forgiveness of our sins. When we are reminded of this, how could we ever withhold this blessing to others?

Have you fully embraced the forgiveness you have in Christ? How has it (or, how has it not) affected the way you forgive others? How does harboring unforgiveness harm your soul?

Day 63: ". . .but if you do not forgive others their trespasses, neither will your Father forgive your trespasses." (6:15)

HERE WE SEE THE severe consequence of an unforgiving heart. A heart that cannot extend forgiveness is one that has not experienced the profound forgiveness, mercy, and grace that God offers us in Jesus Christ. It is a heart gone cold, indifferent to the sin of others, and indifferent to the sin in one-self. Here we find that it is impossible to have a heart transformed by God's redeeming grace and a heart that does not forgive simultaneously. They are mutually exclusive to one another.

So, we must do some honest self-evaluation. We must ask whether we are refusing to forgive someone who has wronged us or hurt us. It may be that we need time before we are ready to forgive someone, and this call to forgiveness does not deny the pain and loss that may be associated with an offense. Yet, there should be no one and nothing to which we state, "I will never forgive." Such a statement can only come from an unrepentant heart that does not know the grace of God in Christ. We may not like this fact, and we may want to clench tightly onto the forgiveness we are with-holding from another. However, to be a disciple of Christ is to relinquish the control we have over who we do and do not forgive. This life that Christ calls us to compels us to be a people so saturated in God's grace that it overflows from our lives to others.

This may be difficult, but sanctification into the image of Christ al-ways is. It cuts deep into the parts of us which we would like to remain unchanged and demands that our lives have a new way of being. This way of being is forgiving, merciful, gracious, and loving. Anything short of it will not do for what God wants to accomplish in our lives. It is slow and tedious work, but by the gift of the Holy Spirit we can be the forgiving people we are created to be. A people whose own transformation in grace is felt by those around us by our mercy and grace. Forgiveness and follow-ing Christ go hand in hand.

Have you checked your heart recently regarding forgiveness? Who might you need to forgive now, and what prevents you from doing so?

Day 64: "And when you fast, do not look gloomy like the hypocrites, for they disfigure their faces that their fasting may be seen by others. Truly, I say to you, they have received their reward." (6:16)

FASTING IS A PRACTICE with which we are not very well acquainted in our modern, Western culture. We live in a society bogged down with consumerism, which perpetually tells us to obtain as much as possible. But, the Master says, "*When* you fast . . . ," not "*If* you fast . . . " Jesus assumes that his disciples will take momentary times to refuse themselves the things of this world so that they might better focus on God and rely on him. This is a discipline that may seem strange to us today, but it does not have to be so. It really can be as simple as skipping a meal to spend time in prayer or turning our phones off for a day so that we might seek God. However, we must also be aware that when we take on the discipline of fasting, it is easy to do it for the wrong reasons as the hypocrites described here do. They do it to be "seen by others," and that is their only reward. When they fast with this improper motivation, they forfeit the reward of the Father who is in heaven.

Likewise, we too might fast so that we seem just a bit more holy than those around us, and it can be one of those things we just casually drop into conversation. We might mention how hungry we are, or how little we use social media, or how we are not dependent on this or that. We can make it a mark of our character, hoping that others view us more highly because of our "devotion." In actuality, this is not devotion at all, but idolatry. We can do this regardless of what we withhold from ourselves as we fast. Whether it be food, technology, television, etc., we can withdraw from these things in unhealthy ways that may actually lead us farther away from God than closer to him. Instead, as followers of Christ, we must be those who are not led away from one thing, only to succumb to other sinful desires. Instead, we pursue Christ wholeheartedly, seeking to become more like him than the things of this world.

Have you fasted before? In what ways did it draw you closer to God? If it didn't, were there any false motivations in your fasting? If you haven't fasted before, would you consider fasting from something in your life to draw closer to God?

Day 65: "But when you fast, anoint your head
and wash your face. . ." (6:17)

THE GOAL OF OUR spiritual practices is not outward "piety," but inward reverence and devotion. The goal is not to be seen for what we do, but for us to better see the God who loves us and calls us to follow him. This means that we need to check our motivations to determine whether our spiritual disciplines stem from pure intentions or are merely outward acts for display. When we find that our spiritual disciplines have become points of pride, we need to take intentional measures to eliminate the showy demonstrations of our faith. We need to anoint our heads and wash our faces so that our spiritual disciplines are seen first and foremost by God, rather than those around us.

This may be particularly true for us with fasting since it is not a discipline we engage in regularly. Therefore, it may be tempting to promote how disciplined and devoted we are by engaging in this practice. However, it may occur with our more regular practices as well. We might easily mention how often we read our Bibles or make sure that everyone sees our hands outstretched in worship, or we may pray long and passionate prayers to garner attention. We can easily do these things simply to portray ourselves as more devoted followers of Christ. When, in actuality, such actions and motivations reveal the opposite.

Such actions reveal that our desire is not God at all, but the praise of others. Thus, we do not do these things to worship God, but with the hopes that others worship us. Functionally, we are attempting to rob God of the praise he deserves. Now, it may be that we read our Bibles often and this comes up in conversation, or we may worship and pray in ways that are passionate and make use of our bodies that are visible to others. But we must be cautious to ensure that the reasons we worship in such ways are truly to praise God, not ourselves. It is too easy and too tempting to make our lives about us when, in reality, the call we have from Christ is one of total self-abandonment. It is a call to lay down our lives so that we may take up Christ's.

Are any of your spiritual disciplines done in a way that is showy, or meant to garner attention? Are your motivations to worship in spirit and in truth (John 4:24), or something else?

Day 66: ". . .that your fasting may not be seen by others but by your Father who is in secret. And your Father who sees in secret will reward you." (6:18)

FASTING IS AN ACT of worship and, therefore, should be directed to God alone. Only he is worthy of such adoration, so it is only the Lord whom we seek to please with our devotion—no one else, including ourselves. Yet, we often find ourselves confused in our devotion. Our devotion is multi-layered, complicated by our own sinfulness, and in need of redemption. Yes, that's right. Even our acts of worship need to be redeemed. Our worship is often plagued with sinfulness, so we must even repent of the ways we have worshipped.

To do so we must become singularly focused, fully devoted to the Lord, and daily seek to draw closer to him. We need to recognize that our only audience for worship is the Lord. When anything else takes his place, we usurp the King of the universe from our hearts and our worship becomes corrupted. Unfortunately, this can often be our default mode of worship. We sit down to read our Bibles or pray, or come to church, or go to a small group with an entire host of fragmented desires that misdirect our worship from the Lord. We need to reset. We need to pause from our practices of devotion and remember who we are worshipping. We need to ask God to reveal the idols within our hearts that are muddled into the ways we approach the Lord.

Ultimately, we need to become more like the Master who was steadfastly devoted to the Father in all things: "So Jesus said to them, "Truly, truly, I say to you, the Son can do nothing of his own accord, but only what he sees the Father doing. For whatever the Father does, that the Son does likewise" (John 5:19). Jesus' entire life was obedient to his Father in devotion, prayer, and deed. Likewise, we too must become devoted in such a manner, following the example of our Savior Jesus Christ who demonstrated perfectly for us what it looks like to pursue the Lord. When we do this, we will find our worship transformed into a rich experience of intimacy with our Father in heaven.

What spiritual practices do you have that may need redemption? How might false motives prevent you from coming to God fully in worship? What changes need to be made?

Day 67: "Do not lay up for yourselves treasures on earth, where moth and rust destroy and where thieves break in and steal. . ." (6:19)

HERE, THE MASTER'S STATEMENT summarizes why we do not practice our righteousness before others (Matt 6:1). It is because, when we do so, we do not lay up for ourselves treasures in heaven, but treasures on earth that will soon pass away. When we put our "righteousness" on display, we trade the reward of heaven from our Father for the reward of this world from our peers. Such earthly rewards are vastly fleeting.

Rather, we must seek to cultivate inner righteousness. This is not a righteousness of our own making. By no means! It is the pursuit of righteousness without show. Inner righteousness is quiet piety and humble devotion to the Lord that is unconcerned about whether we receive the praise of others or not. By seeking the Lord in this manner, we are rewarded with the eternal treasures of heaven that do not pass away. So, when we give, pray, or fast, we must be certain that we do not put on a ceremonious display. But, instead, a discreet action that seeks the approval of our Father in heaven alone. It must be worship devoted to the Lord himself, instead of ourselves or others, and it is only in this way that we might store up heavenly treasure.

This might lead us to wonder about the treasures we are storing up. What do they look like? Is it treasure that is susceptible to rust and decay? Or, perhaps a better question, would we be content if this earthly treasure were taken away from us? Are we willing to be devoted to the Lord even if no one knows, cares, or pays attention? Would we follow Christ even if no one applauds us for doing so! When we think upon these questions, we might feel the conviction that our religious devotion is often just to keep up appearances. When we realize this, we must come to the conclusion that there is serious repentance that needs to take place in our lives. What better way to do this than to go into our rooms, pray quietly for forgiveness, and once again seek the heavenly treasures the Father has in store for us.

Which treasure do you value most, that which can be seen here on earth or that which you hope for in Heaven? How might a heavenly mindset of treasure reshape the way you practice spiritual disciplines such as prayer, fasting, and giving?

Day 68: ". . .but lay up for yourselves treasures in heaven, where neither moth nor rust destroys and where thieves do not break in and steal." (6:20)

GREATER THAN THE TREASURES this world has to offer are those of heaven from the Father. Not only do they surpass earthly treasures in value, but in longevity, lasting for all eternity and enjoyable forever. Yet, we are still so prone to forsake these heavenly gifts for temporary moments of satisfaction and praise. We know what is good, and we might even want it, but the allure of earthly treasure diverts our gaze and corrupts our attempts to honor the Lord. This verse reminds us that we must forsake the earthly treasures that distract us.

When we think of the context in which Jesus spoke these words, we see that laying up heavenly treasure is rather straightforward. It is praying, giving to the needy, and fasting. That's it; it's that simple. However, these acts of devotion come with a stipulation, and the acts themselves are not the sole basis for determining their worth. For, it is who our audience is that determines whether the fruit of our spiritual disciplines is heavenly or earthly. If our audience is our Father in Heaven, then we store up for ourselves heavenly treasure. If our audience is those around us, then we'll only receive earthly praise. We might think storing up heavenly treasure is just for those who are "extra spiritual," but those who appear "extra spiritual" may, in fact, only be storing up earthly treasures.

Heavenly treasure is instead for the meek, humble, and contrite in heart. Those who seek God and his will, whether others are watching or not. The recipients of heavenly treasure are the men and women who pray with an earnest heart in the privacy of their own homes. It is for those who abstain from material goods to focus on the Lord without needing to be affirmed by their peers. It is for the anonymous donors, not professional philanthropists, who may only give a few dollars, but in doing so ensure that someone has their next meal covered. It is these whom Christ says are laying up for themselves an imperishable treasure that will persist throughout all eternity. Isn't that worth so much more than a few words of praise from our peers?

How might you better cultivate spiritual disciplines that seek heavenly treasure instead of earthly treasure? When you do pray/give/fast publicly (which is fine), how might you do so in ways that are still seeking the treasures of heaven over those of the earth?

Day 69: "For where your treasure is, there your heart will be also." (6:21)

THE TYPE OF TREASURE we are seeking immediately tells us about our motivations, our intentions, and our hearts. If we are seeking earthly treasures, that is precisely where our hearts are. They are focused on worldly, temporal, and ultimately fleeting things. The saddest thing of all is that, when our hearts are set on obtaining these things, we are usually successful. Our hearts truly are where our treasure lies.

This is not to say that the things of this world are inherently bad, unimportant, and unnecessary. We do need financial stability, affirmation, community, and so forth. But, when those things become the ultimate goal, then the desires of our hearts have become misplaced. Likewise, our hearts can become comfortable with the habitat of earthly praise and reward, rather than God's glory and heavenly rewards. Oddly, when all is said and done, we won't even care about the earthly praises we have received over our lifetimes.

I remember the last time I walked out of my high school at 18 years old. I reflected on the four years I had spent trying to make friends, be well-liked, and to fit in with my peers. I had so desperately wanted the acceptance of others and to belong that I would have done just about anything to obtain these things. Oddly, as I walked down the main hallway and out of the building for the last time, none of that mattered. I didn't care whatsoever what my peers had thought of me. Every awkward encounter or attempt at social advancement where I sought the approval of others evaporated in an instant. I was instead thinking about much bigger and more important things that were ahead.

So, will it be when we come to the final moments of our lives here on earth. The wealth we accrue, the social spheres we run in, and the accolades we have received; these won't matter in our final moments before we are lowered into the dirt. What will matter is the kingdom we will walk into and the treasures we have stored up there. These treasures are stored up when the inclinations of our hearts are towards the Lord and not ourselves. We must perpetually abandon ourselves to pursue God. When we do so, we will find ourselves inhabiting the glory of heaven, surrounded by the abundant and everlasting treasure the Father desires to give us.

Where is your treasure? Where is your heart? Does a change need to be made in your life regarding what you treasure?

Day 70: "The eye is the lamp of the body. So, if your eye is healthy, your whole body will be full of light. . ." (6:22)

THIS VERSE, AND THE next, are some of the more confusing ones that we find in the Sermon. The basic point in discussing the eye is to address how we interact with the world around us. What do we lay our eyes on, and on what do we fix our gaze? What emotions are stirred up within us when we look at one thing or another? Do we covet? Are we envious? Greedy? Lustful? Disdainful? Disgusted? The key thing to note is that what is external to ourselves, what we see and place our eyes upon, has effects within us. If you recall Matthew 5:28, Jesus says that a lustful gaze, looking at something external, leads to adultery internally.

This verse is serving as an extension of what Jesus has spoken about since the beginning of chapter 6, asking us once again to reevaluate where our hearts and treasure are. Where we fix our eyes and devote our attention is descriptive of what is taking place within us and reveals the true desires of our hearts. Of course, this doesn't mean that we don't ever look at anything around us. But we must pay attention to what occurs within us when we observe the things that might entice us. When we can be among things that we might desire, but keep our gaze upon heavenly and eternal things, then our eyes are healthy and we are filled with light.

That is what Christ is calling us to in his sermon, to be focused on the Kingdom of Heaven amid the world in which we live. That doesn't mean that we ignore or despise the material things that make up this life. Instead, we seek Christ's kingdom and weigh our desires based upon what eternally matters rather than what will pass away. This is what should hold our attention and be our greatest desire. Though we need the physical things of this world, these things should never hold the weight of all our hopes and desires. Only the Lord and his kingdom are worthy of such hopes, and only Christ can fulfill them.

Are you full of the light of the Kingdom of Heaven, or does something else hold your gaze? What might you need to divert your gaze from to follow Christ more wholeheartedly?

Day 71: ". . .but if your eye is bad, your whole body will be full of darkness. If then the light in you is darkness, how great is the darkness!" (6:23)

THE PSALMIST TELLS US, "Those who make [idols] become like them; so do all who trust in them" (Ps 115:8). It's no secret that the things we long for most become the very things that define us. If the things our eyes desire are of darkness, then that is exactly what we will be as well: full of darkness and having no light. If we desire to amass tremendous amounts of wealth and succeed at it, we'll be known for our money but probably little else. If we desire fame and popularity, we might be well known, but we will not be known well. If we desire to have power and influence, it's unlikely we will be known for our kindness and servanthood.

We can desire all these things and be consumed by them, allowing them to push God aside from his place as ruler over our lives. However, if we keep our eyes focused on the things of God and his kingdom, we will be full of light, displaying the qualities that define the kingdom. We'll be merciful and gracious people who give, not to be seen, but to serve those in need with humility. We'll be prayerful people who delight in communing with the Lord instead of delighting in how pious we may appear to others. We'll be fasting people who are more concerned about being filled with the Spirit than with the pleasures of the world.

As we do this, we'll become more and more satisfied with the things of heaven, rather than the things of this world. We'll be full of light that is on display for the world to lead others towards the Lord. What we seek and desire is truly what we become. Just as the Psalmist says, we become like the very things we worship. If it is the worldly things that pass away, then so shall we. But, if it is the eternal treasures of heaven that are found through our devotion to Christ, then it is he who we become like.

What desires do you have that you are becoming more like? Are they full of light or darkness? How might you better pursue things that are light?

Day 72: "No one can serve two masters, for either he will hate the one and love the other, or he will be devoted to the one and despise the other. You cannot serve God and money." (6:24)

WE TEND TO THINK that we can have or do it all. Yet, time and time again, experience tells us that our lives and our loyalties are divided. We fail to uphold commitments, we break promises, and we neglect important things in our lives. The Master is calling us to be singular in our devotion. Our whole selves must be fully devoted to following Christ and pursuing his kingdom. Anything that comes before this divides our allegiance and diminishes our ability to follow Christ as he would have us.

Money is the example here, and we all know how much money can divert our devotions. We are easily swayed by it in our culture, and every decision is usually weighed against the almighty dollar. We speak of what makes financial sense or results in the largest net gain, and we seldom ask what God would have us do with our finances. If we do ask the latter question, we still often choose what is most financially lucrative. However, Christ is calling us here to an allegiance that cannot be purchased. An allegiance that is so steadfast that all the wealth in the world could not sway us from our pursuit of God. There is one Master and no other in the Christian's life. Without a doubt, this is a difficult path to follow.

So, how do we manage the things that demand our attention, such as our spouse, children, careers, and so forth? Of course, Christ's call does not mean that we pay no attention to such things. Rather, it means that we pursue him in all these things as well. We love Christ, and therefore sacrificially love our spouses and family. We love Christ, and therefore we carry out our vocation as though we are working for him. Brothers and sisters, it is in our undivided love for Christ that we find we can truly love others and best carry out our responsibilities. Christ is our Master, and to please the Master we love as he loves, give as he gives, and serve as he serves. When we do so, our allegiance is singular, but the blessing to ourselves and others are many.

Who is truly your master? Who or what do you serve above all else? Is it Christ, or something in his place?

Day 73: "Therefore I tell you, do not be anxious about your life, what you will eat or what you will drink, nor about your body, what you will put on. Is not life more than food, and the body more than clothing?" (6:25)

IF CHRIST, RATHER THAN money, is our Master, then our anxieties should not be earthly things. The person who serves money will become bogged down with the weight of worry over earthly things, but not the person who serves Christ. This is not to say that food, water, and clothing are unimportant. Of course they are! The point is that Jesus knows perfectly well that we need these things, yet he still calls us to follow him above even our daily needs. This does not mean that we neglect our daily needs and are completely unmindful of them, but that our first desire is Christ above all.

The verse is rather easy for us in the Western world to swallow. Typically, we do not need to worry about the source of our next meal. We turn on the tap, and there is water. We open the pantry, and there is food. We open a closet, and it's full of clothing. Others around the world do not know such luxuries. And yes, these are luxuries. Many around the world, and in the U.S., must trust in the Lord to provide such daily needs. For people in these situations, Jesus' words might even seem cruel. How are the poor not supposed to worry about such things? Remember, Jesus himself and the people he is speaking to in the Sermon are not unfamiliar with such situations. They knew what it is to truly hunger and thirst. Jesus is not trying to be cruel to his audience at all. Jesus is saying that even if we need such things, we should still have a greater desire to inherit the Kingdom of Heaven than to inherit the things of this life.

For those of us who do not have to worry about our physical needs, I suggest that we are still anxious about them in other ways. We worry about how well we will eat and drink, or how nice and trendy the clothes are that we will wear. My friends, this is worrying all the same. When these things come before Christ and his kingdom, they are idols in our lives. Therefore, dear Christian—whether rich or poor, well-fed or hungry, quenched or thirsty, clothed or naked—let us all first seek Christ and allow secondary things to remain secondary.

In what ways do you worry about food, drink, or clothing? Do you worry about what you lack, or the quality of what you possess?

Day 74: "Look at the birds of the air: they neither sow nor reap nor gather into barns, and yet your heavenly Father feeds them. Are you not of more value than they?" (6:26)

WE TEND TO FORGET that we possess value before our Maker, we matter to him. Though we are sinful and lack righteousness apart from Christ, God has created us in his image and endowed us with his breath of life. You, dear friend, possess worth before the Lord of the universe! It is not a worth we find in and of ourselves, but worth that stems from the creator of the universe. It stems from the one who possesses all worthiness and deems what else in existence possesses worth. The value we possess stems from the source of all worth.

Along with our worth comes God's providential care, which is unique for humanity. God loves us fiercely and cares for us graciously. We might read this verse and think we do not need to work. Or, if we are true followers of Christ, all our needs will be met. This is a false teaching that stems from the prosperity gospel, which we must wholly reject. This false gospel suggests that if we possess enough faith we will be blessed with health and material gain, and many have suggested that this verse affirms such teaching. But we must remember that the Sermon speaks of a kingdom that is both *here* and *not yet* fully manifest. Christ has presently ushered in the Kingdom of Heaven through his life, death, and resurrection. However, the fullest expressions of the kingdom are *not yet* present. In the *here*, we experience some of the blessings of the kingdom, but these blessings still exist within a sinful and fallen world.

So, when Jesus tells his audience that they have more value than the birds of the air, he is not saying their daily sustenance is simply going to fall into their laps. On occasions, the Lord's provision can operate in unique and miraculous ways, but it is not the norm. In the wider context of this verse, we see that Jesus is telling his disciples where their hope should be fixed. He is, once again, suggesting that they should have one master in their lives, and it is the Lord alone. It is he who will truly and fully provide. When Christ comes again, we will see the fullest expression of Christ's words come to fruition. Until that time, we hope in the Lord, knowing that he cares for us in ways beyond our imagination.

How trusting of God are you for your day-to-day needs? Do you rely more on yourself, or on God for the things you need in life?

Day 75: "And which of you by being anxious can
add a single hour to his span of life?" (6:27)

JESUS' QUESTION IS STRAIGHTFORWARD. It penetrates to the core of who
we are at times. We believe that we can worry ourselves through a situation or difficult circumstance. We fall into this trap all the time, believing that if we mentally anguish over something long enough, we'll find
solutions on the other side. However, instead of solutions, we find ourselves exhausted, often hopeless, and in the exact same place we started.
Being anxious is not the same thing as thinking about things that deserve
thought. Rather, it is dwelling on things in an unhealthy way, allowing
what we are thinking about to consume us.

Essentially, anxiousness is thinking without trust. Let me point out
that I am not talking about clinical anxiety or implying those who experience anxiety this way do not trust in the Lord. I believe what is being
discussed here is the generic type of anxiousness we all encounter, or even
invite, into our lives regularly. This sort of anxiousness is being concerned
about what we will eat, drink, or wear while failing to remember that we
have a gracious and loving Father watching over us. It is thinking about
everything to be accomplished for the day without submitting our plans to
the Lord. It is thinking that we must find a solution to our problems while
failing to recognize that God is sovereignly ruling over everything. This
way of thinking produces absolutely nothing. It is unproductive thought,
spinning wheels that move us nowhere.

Furthermore, the anxieties we carry are often disproportional to the
things that we are concerned about. When this happens, we are overbur-
dened by the concerns of this world and are sapped of joy. We tend to be like
Martha in Luke 10, anxiously running about taking care of all the details that
need attending. All the while, our gracious Master is sitting there waiting for
us to come to him. So, we must learn to pause. We need to learn to reflect
in those moments of anxiety and look to God. We'll then see how he has
provided and cared for us in the past, and we'll see how he will continue to
care for us in the future. When we do this, friend, we allow the Lord to take
all the burdens we carry off our shoulders and place them on himself. Then,
we are in a much better position to pursue the things God has laid before us.

*Are you anxious? What about? Has your anxiety produced anything
for you? What will it look like to turn the things you are anxious
about over to the Lord?*

75

Day 76: "And why are you anxious about clothing?
Consider the lilies of the field, how they grow:
they neither toil nor spin. . ." (6:28)

EACH MORNING I STARE into a closet full of clothing and wonder what I will wear. I wonder which shirt to pair with which pants, and which belt and shoes, and how all the styles and colors will work together. I wonder how I will be perceived by others in this combination of fabric hanging from my body. When I think of this verse in conjunction with my morning routine, I realize that my anxieties over clothing are incredibly selfish. They are all about how I will look and how others will see me. I don't even necessarily want to stand out, but I do want others to at least make positive assumptions about me based on the way I'm dressed.

As I've mentioned before, most of us in the Western world have anxiety over our abundance, not over our lack. Unlike Jesus' original audience, we do not wonder if we will have anything to wear at all, but whether we will wear the right thing. Yet, in either case, the Master tells us not to worry about such things. He tells us that we have a caring Father who loves us and is watching over us. He tells us we are the work of a Creator who could have made a bland world, lacking in color and beauty, but he instead chose to fill it with flowers, plants, and trees of every shape and color. When we keep this as our perspective, we can begin to worry less about the day-to-day needs that God is watching over.

In all this, Jesus is teaching us to be content and still. He is teaching us what unwavering faith in the Lord looks like. He is teaching us to possess a faith that is so trusting that we can be like the flowers of the field who do not work to adorn themselves so beautifully. This is the kind of faith that the Master is calling us to have in all things, whether our concerns be food, drink, or clothing. In all things, Jesus is telling us that there is something of much greater value that should be on our hearts and minds. When we are distracted by the material things of this world, we might miss it entirely.

Do you worry about clothing regularly? Do you attach your image and how you are perceived to your self-worth? How might Jesus' words here teach us to find our self-worth in God alone and not the things of this world?

Day 77: ". . .yet I tell you, even Solomon in all his glory was not arrayed like one of these." (6:29)

THIS VERSE TEACHES US that God can more beautifully clothe a field than a person can dress themself. Solomon was exceedingly wealthy and likely wore only the finest clothing for his day. Yet it still paled in comparison to the rest of creation. Ironically, it is people like Solomon whom we may be tempted to envy when it comes to clothing. In our current digital age and prolific (and troubling) use of social media, we can mindlessly gawk at the styles and fashions of celebrities. When we do, we may become envious of their wealth and access to the poshest brands. We can easily see what everyone else is wearing and become jealous of the styles available to an elite few.

However, even these celebrities in their designer brands are not dressed nearly as beautifully as the grass of the field. What God can do in his creation far exceeds our ability to manipulate and manufacture materials for our own clothing. We may think that our creativity or use of modern materials and weaving together of synthetic fabrics is what it means to be beautifully dressed. However, it is God's infinite creativity that makes the entire world around us beautiful. Moreover, it is the Lord's infinite creativity and workings within this world that give beauty and value to anything in this world at all. The things we see and call beautiful are only so because God has made them in such a way and gifted them with beauty.

Thus, it is God who ultimately determines what is beautiful, including clothing. I am confident that we naturally resonate with this truth. Just think about it. Have you ever seen a field bursting with flowers and color and were simply awestruck? Probably so. Have you ever seen someone's outfit and had the same reaction? Probably not. That's because there is no comparison. Most importantly, this verse recognizes God's provision for the creation he loves so dearly. When we read these verses, we should be encouraged, knowing that God has concern for our most basic and fundamental needs, including clothing. After all, it is God himself who first clothed humanity when we were in our moment of greatest need, "And the Lord God made for Adam and for his wife garments of skins and clothed them" (Gen 3:21).

Are you ever concerned that your clothing isn't good enough? Are you tempted to compare your clothing to other individuals? Do you trust in the Lord to provide for this need?

Day 78: "But if God so clothes the grass of the field, which today is alive and tomorrow is thrown into the oven, will he not much more clothe you, O you of little faith?" (6:30)

WE ARE JUST LIKE the disciples to whom Jesus spoke these words; we are a people of "little faith." Like those who first followed the Master, we need constant reminders of God's gracious provision here on earth. We look at our lives, but we tend to do so from a pessimist's perspective. We view our lives like they are the proverbial half-empty glass, lacking the things we want and desire. And, we do this while failing to look around at all the subtle ways God is caring for us and keeping our glasses half-full. We open closets that have plenty of clothing, yet we can quite easily see how it could be fuller or filled with better brands. We open fridges with more than enough food, yet we wish there were a few more choice items for us to pick from.

Basically, we only consider how God provides for us individually while failing to see how God has provided for the whole earth, the grass of the field included. We fail to see God's care for the creatures that roam the forests, plains, deserts, and oceans. God has graciously woven into creation a beautiful balance to care for all of life on earth. However, the second we are lacking one thing, God's providential care is called into question. It is because we, just like the disciples, possess "little faith" in the Lord who presides over the universe.

So, we need to be reminded again to look around at God's care for his creation. We simply need to look to the fields that are dressed in flowers to be encouraged that God is looking down from his throne with the utmost care. As we read this verse, we should also be reminded that to see God's care and provision is much easier for us than for many. Others can read this verse, like Jesus' original audience, with exceedingly greater needs than we have. Many read this verse who do not have a full closet or pantry and wonder if these words can really be true. If that is not us, then perhaps we are a part of the answer to this verse. Rather than question whether this verse is true in our own lives, instead, we should seek to fulfill it in the lives of others.

Do you tend to look at God's provision only on your terms and not based on God's provision for all of creation? How might you be the fulfillment of this verse for others?

Day 79: "Therefore do not be anxious, saying, 'What shall we eat?' or 'What shall we drink?' or 'What shall we wear?'" (6:31)

HAVING COMPLETE TRUST IN the Lord and being anxious about the things of life are a tension every follower of Christ faces. We know in our hearts that God is good and cares for us. But, in just one moment, our beliefs can be turned upside-down by the demands of life and call into question what we know to be true about God. Thus, we need this reminder to not be anxious. We need the ever-calming words of Christ to affirm once again that God does indeed love and care for us and does so more deeply than we could ever begin to imagine. This verse is not suggesting that we do not care whether we will have food, drink, or clothing. Instead, it tells us that we should not allow our thoughts to be dominated by even the routine things we need in life.

Yes, we do need all three of these things daily, but our trust in God should lead us to seek him and his kingdom above all earthly things. Just for a moment, imagine if you spent as much time thinking about the Lord as you do about food, drink, and clothing? Do you think it might realign the priorities in your life and change the way you live? What might it do to give these things over to the Lord in prayer rather than dwelling on them throughout the day? Now, of course, it is much easier said than done to simply stop worrying about these things and begin focusing on the Lord. We might succeed for a moment, or even a day or so, but then the regular demands of life slap us in the face and divert our attention.

So maybe the solution isn't so much in ignoring food, drink, and clothing but in learning to trust God in these things and handing them over to him. It is the daily practice of laying down our burdens at the foot of the cross, trusting in the one who has provided for our greatest need to continue to sustain us from moment to moment. Friend, isn't our hope in heaven so much greater than the anxieties of this life?

How might you lay down your concerns about daily needs? More importantly, are you willing to lay down your worries for the things you need daily? Does a lack of trust in God prevent you from doing so?

Day 80: "For the Gentiles seek after all these things, and your heavenly Father knows that you need them all." (6:32)

To follow the Master, we must determine whether we will pursue him or the things the world does. This is not to say we don't seek the things we need in life, but it does mean that we are not consumed by these things, nor are they our passion. Our passion is Christ alone, it is him we seek above all else. We must pursue Christ with undivided devotion, knowing that all of our needs are seen by our Father above. He is sovereignly watching from above with the heart of a Father who desires the best for his children.

To follow Christ is to place unwavering and steadfast hope in God the Father, just as Christ routinely relied on the Father and sought him throughout his life. Will there be times of lack and need? Certainly! It is no doubt that Christ was much more well acquainted with times of need than you or I. Yet, his trust was undeterred, and he continually relied on the Father—even as he was led on the arduous journey to the cross. Likewise, in our own moments of difficulty, God is with us. He is our Father. He is not an absentee God who looks on from a safe distance. No! He is loving and compassionate and responsive to the needs of his children. Therefore, it is him we should run to when we face difficult moments and trials, not the things of this life that we think will satisfy the desires of our hearts.

We must be ever vigilant to ask ourselves what we are truly seeking in this life. What do we really want? Is it wealth? Security? Health? Influence? These things are good in and of themselves, but set these above the Lord, and you may find them to your own demise. You may amass a great fortune, a "perfect" body, or all the prestige the world has to offer. But, if they have come before the Lord, they will bankrupt and rob your soul just as they have for countless others. Friends, let it not be so with us. The peoples of every nation seek these things, but let us, the citizens of Christ's kingdom, engage in pursuits with eternal significance.

What are you seeking? How are your desires a reflection of your trust in God's provision? Do you live as if God will not provide, or do you trust him to do so?

Day 81: "But seek first the kingdom of God and his righteousness, and all these things will be added to you." (6:33)

THIS VERSE IS THE climax to what Jesus began saying back in verse 25. It represents the defining principle for how we order our lives and give priority to our desires. The defining principle is to seek the Kingdom of God above all things. The Sermon is teaching us what it looks like to seek Christ's kingdom, which we cannot begin to do if other desires supplant our love for the Lord and his kingdom. But when we do live as citizens of Christ's kingdom, a beautiful promise comes along with that pursuit: that our secondary needs will be filled.

Now, this verse has been misused by suggesting that those who lack material things are not truly seeking the kingdom, and those who are materially blessed really are. This, once again, is the ever-rampant heresy in the church today that is called the prosperity gospel. So, we must remember that the Sermon is speaking both about the present and the future. The Sermon exists in the *here* and *not yet* realities of Christ's kingdom. It is *here* in Christ's life and ministry and evident within the church, but it is *not yet* fully visible. We get ourselves into trouble when we seek the promises of the *not yet* in the *here and now*. When we assume that we can claim the future blessings of the kingdom in the present we have overstepped Jesus' teachings and the full witness of Scripture.

Yes, if we seek the kingdom, we will have everything we could ever hope for or desire at Christ's return and the full establishment of his kingdom. However, in the present, we may still experience moments of need and want. This does not mean that we are not seeking the kingdom or do not possess enough faith. It means that we are still living in a fallen and broken world where evil has *not yet* been fully expelled. So, as we trudge on in life, we do seek the kingdom! We do so full of hope, knowing that our good and gracious Father is bringing about his purposes in this world where all that our hearts could ever hope for will be added to us.

Do you trust that God is bringing about his kingdom where all your needs will be met? Or, do you struggle to believe that God could provide for the things you need in this life? What keeps you from trusting in him?

Day 82: "Therefore do not be anxious about tomorrow, for tomorrow will be anxious for itself. Sufficient for the day is its own trouble." (6:34)

WE TEND TO DWELL on things. Whether that be things present or things to come, we make a habit of worrying and allowing things beyond our control to consume our thoughts. Every aspect of life can come crashing into our minds, increasing our worry and anxiety and may even lead to depression. For some reason, despite previous failed attempts, we believe we can think our way out of anxiousness. We hope that, with enough mental exertion, we can overcome the things that occupy our thoughts. Yet, this tends to add to our anxieties rather than alleviate them. This is true for many of us today, and we'll find it to be true tomorrow as well.

So, Jesus' advice seems a little strange here: "do not be anxious." In my experience, being told, "don't be anxious," does little to relieve my anxiety. So, what is the Master after here? Notice that Jesus is not saying to never be anxious. We all have anxiety at times, and this is just a fact of life. Jesus is, however, saying not to be anxious "about tomorrow." Jesus knows us well. He knows that we can get a bit ahead of ourselves from time to time. He knows that the things that give us anxiety can outpace what we can address in the current moment. He knows that we tend to worry about things that lie in the future, even though we have not resolved what is presently before us.

Jesus' words remind us to slow down. Take things one day at a time, rather than trying to clear every hurdle of life in a single leap. Start by addressing the things that are immediately before you instead of fretting about the things that must be dealt with tomorrow. Today already has enough anxiety, so don't add tomorrow's anxiety onto today as well. Tomorrow will come with its own trouble, so deal with it then and allow yourself to focus on today's troubles. My friend, you and I are prone to get ahead of ourselves. Thankfully, Christ's words remind us that we do not have to solve every problem immediately. Navigating life and patiently pursuing the Master is something we accomplish one day at a time.

Do you tend to be anxious about more than you can handle in a single moment? How can you slow down to focus on what is at hand rather than what is forthcoming? How might taking things one day at a time help relieve some of your anxiety?

Day 83: "Judge not, that you be not judged." (7:1)

WITHOUT A SHADOW OF a doubt, this is the most abused verse in the entire Bible. I don't have particular statistics to back up that claim, but the number of times I've seen these words carelessly thrown around is significantly more than for any other verse. Though this devotional is treating the Sermon verse-by-verse, we cannot forget that Jesus did not stop speaking immediately after these words. They come within the context of a bigger idea. We might read these words and think we should never make any judgments about another individual, whatsoever. However, this is not what Jesus is saying.

Certainly, we do not judge the eternal state of other people, that is never our role. However, as Paul states in 1 Corinthians, his job is not to judge those outside the church, but it certainly is to judge those within it (1 Cor 5:12). Typically, this verse is tossed about casually, suggesting that we should never call anything sinful, but this fails to take into account all of what the Master is teaching us. Routinely in the Sermon Jesus is addressing hypocrisy, calling out those who wear masks concealing their inward hearts and motivations. He is addressing (you might even say judging) those whose actions, motivations, and character are not in sync with one another. Those who would call something sinful, yet who engage in the very same sin they shame and condemn in others. This is not a call for us to abandon calling sin a "sin," but a demand for us to look within ourselves and measure our own actions, motivations, and character.

So, it is not that we ignore the sin in others by any means. Instead, we must first evaluate the sinfulness in our own lives. When we do this, we will find ourselves in a much humbler position, recognizing that we may not be in a place to address another person's sin. As Paul says in Romans 2:22, "you who say that one must not commit adultery, do you commit adultery? You who abhor idols, do you rob temples?" It is questions like these that must be asked first before addressing the sin of another. When we do this, we can begin to take the masks we all wear off, removing the hypocrisy in our own lives before calling our brothers and sisters to holiness.

Do you ever find yourself judging first, without evaluating your own life and sins? Are you tempted to be overly judgmental, or entirely lax in addressing other's sins?

Day 84: "For with the judgment you pronounce you will be judged, and with the measure you use it will be measured to you." (7:2)

THIS VERSE PROVIDES THE reason why we should be careful to judge others: how we judge others is how we will be judged. If we judge others for lying, we will be judged on the integrity of our own speech. If we judge others for stealing, we will be judged on how honestly we have gained our wealth. If we judge others for any sin, we will be judged on whether we have committed the very same sin. When we evaluate our own lives in light of this, we might find that our lips ought to be sealed more often than not. Again, this verse and the previous one are not commands to never address the sin in others or to correct those who are at fault. Jesus teaches the opposite to his disciples later in the Gospel of Matthew (Matt 18:15-17).

Instead, the Master is calling for us to evaluate our own lives with scrutiny. Whatever sins we find in ourselves—which we all have plenty—are the areas where we should refrain from judging others. To do so is to invite judgment back upon ourselves, receiving the measure we used with others for ourselves. When we learn this, we see how much humility we ought to have in our lives. We learn that the thing we share most in common with the rest of humanity is that we are indeed sinful. But, addressing sin must always begin with ourselves, not others. Whenever we do address faults in others, we must be ever careful to show grace and mercy as well.

Think of your own struggles with various sins. Would you like to have a brother or sister come screaming at you and condemning you, pouring judgment upon you for faults of which you are aware? Or, would you rather they approach you graciously and lovingly, hoping for you to grow as a person and in your devotion to the Lord? If you are like me, you would prefer the friend who approaches you with grace. Yet, we may still be quick to judge others and to do so mercilessly. So, perhaps, we should already be mindful of Christ's forthcoming words, "whatever you wish that others would do to you, do also to them" (Matt 7:12).

Are you guilty of the sins you condemn in others? Do you hold others to standards you do not apply to yourself? What does repentance look like in such scenarios?

Day 85: "Why do you see the speck that is in your brother's eye, but do not notice the log that is in your own eye?" (7:3)

WE ARE PRONE TO hypocrisy. We quickly see everything that is wrong in another yet fail to deal with our very own shortcomings. We are often blinded by pride, or another sin, to the point that we think we see clearly. In reality, we regularly judge others for things that apply to us as well. Unfortunately, this is often our human nature. We assume everyone is in the wrong but ourselves.

Recognizing that we are apt to do this is the first step in renewal. Once we realize that we do not have it all together, that we do fall short of the mark and have sin in our lives, then we can begin to address the faults within ourselves. We start to see that, though there is sin in those around us, there is an ample amount in our own lives we need to deal with first. We all have logs hanging out of our eye sockets, perfectly visible to those around us, yet glaringly absent from our own vision. We need to have our vision renewed and begin an honest appraisal of our lives, taking stock of who and what we are. We must take the difficult questions we might put toward others and point them toward ourselves. Doing so, we may recognize what our own particular logs may be, and we will also be humbled in the process. We like to think the log in our eye is much smaller than our brother or sister's, but when we begin to deal honestly with ourselves, we find a much larger piece of timber.

After we have recognized our own sin and appraised ourselves honestly, then begins the difficult road of repentance, removing the log from our own eyes. This is painful and difficult work. This is where we actually have to deal with our shortcomings and, quite often, remove the sins in our lives that we use as defense systems or coping mechanisms. They are quite often things we like, love, or make us feel safe. Though Christ accepts us for who we are, he is not content to leave us there. He desires that we become all that he has created us to be, and he will leave no sin in us that prevents us from becoming just that.

In what ways do you see other peoples' sins, but neglect your own? Take a moment and reflect on what logs may be in your eye. What did you find? What needs to be done?

Day 86: "Or how can you say to your brother, 'Let me take the speck out of your eye,' when there is the log in your own eye?" (7:4)

IT IS ALWAYS TEMPTING to try and fix other peoples' problems rather than address our own. Calling out the faults in others is much easier than recognizing the shortcomings we have within ourselves. Instead of doing the hard and painstaking work of trying to better ourselves, we like to turn others into improvement projects so that they are more suitable to us. We do this, thinking that if everyone around us somehow got it together, everything would be just fine. Of course, then, we would not need to change ourselves at all.

We are, quite frankly, oblivious to our own sin. Yet, we are still somehow aware that it lurks behind the scenes at the same time. We know it's there, but we pretend that it is not. Though we all know we are sinful, we still tend to think we are never at fault. We are overly critical of others' faults, but we are forgiving of our own. To use Jesus' terminology in the Sermon, we are hypocrites. So, what must we do? Well, foremost, we must have an inward shift concerning how we view others and how we see ourselves. We ought to measure equally, working diligently to remove the bias we have towards ourselves. We must judge others with the same fairness and forgiveness we apply to ourselves and with the fairness and forgiveness we would like from others.

Furthermore, we must also address the log so surreptitiously lodged in our eye so that we can serve our brothers and sisters. It would be much easier to leave the log in our eye, and this is the route some take. Some choose to not address their own sin or the sin of others, presuming upon the grace of the Lord while denying his holiness and justice. Granted, this is a route that is fair towards ourselves and others. However, this still fails to live up to what the Sermon demands. To embrace the commands of the Sermon is to recognize the sin we have in ourselves and remove it. Then we may also address the sins that pull down our brothers and sisters.

Just as we asked yesterday, what logs are in your eye that need to be addressed? Think deeply, are there ones that are hidden from your sight? Are there sins you purposefully ignore?

Day 87: "You hypocrite, first take the log out of your own eye, and then you will see clearly to take the speck out of your brother's eye." (7:5)

Throughout the Old Testament, God judges the nations. Often, when this occurs, the judgment begins with the chosen people of Israel before the other nations are judged. Peter states, similarly, "For it is time for judgment to begin at the household of God; and if it begins with us, what will be the outcome for those who do not obey the gospel of God?" (1 Pet 4:17) So too should it be when we address sinfulness; we must begin in-house and with ourselves. It is our sinfulness that should be given priority, not the sinfulness of others. Oddly, we often invert this and begin with other's sins before our own. Or, worse, we judge others and never address our sins at all.

My friends, if we are to follow the Master, then this cannot be. We cannot allow for such deviation from Christ's teaching. We must, for the sake of our own souls and the encouragement of our brothers and sisters in the faith, come to terms with our sins and seek to rectify the areas where we fail. We will likely find ourselves busy enough with this task that we do not even have time remaining to address the sins of those around us. We all have within us an ample number of shortcomings where we fail to miss the mark of what the Lord requires. And, we cannot be fooled, it is holiness that God requires of us (1 Pet 1:15-16). When we realize that this is the standard that God desires, we should become acutely aware that we have an exceeding amount of log removal to do from our eyes.

Of course, we cannot achieve this standard of holiness on our own and apart from Christ. However, we are not permitted to use our inability to be holy as an excuse for sin. Instead, we strive with the aid of the Holy Spirit living in us to live lives more in conformity to God's Word each day. When we do this, we begin to make small and meaningful steps towards removing the logs in our eyes. It's hard work and slow progress, but the daily steps we take in sanctification are always worth it.

One more time: What logs may be in your eye that need to be removed? Are you willing to remove them? Why or why not? What is one tangible step you can take to begin addressing one thing now?

Day 88: "Do not give dogs what is holy, and do not throw your pearls before pigs, lest they trample them underfoot and turn to attack you." (7:6)

MUCH OF THE SERMON is clear and straightforward. Here, however, Jesus' words are a bit more cryptic and difficult to understand. There are a few options that have been suggested for how to read this verse. First, it may be that Jesus is speaking about taking the gospel to the Gentiles, and this would fit in with other parts of Matthew's Gospel (Matt 15:21-28). Second, the Sermon also confronts the ways that the scribes and Pharisees have misread the law and failed to truly live out its spirit. It may be that his words here are addressing how the disciples should abstain from interacting with such groups whatsoever. These are both reasonable explanations, but the first explanation does not seem to fit within the Sermon itself. The latter interpretation seems inconsistent with the verse that comes immediately before.

There is at least one more possibility worth considering. We have just read the words, "do not judge," so the temptation may be to step back and withhold all judgment from our brothers and sisters. Or, on the contrary (and much more likely!), we may self-righteously overstep the boundaries regarding whom we may judge and correct. This verse seems to be working to curb our desire to judge beyond our limits. A proper reprimand can indeed be a good, holy, and necessary thing (Prov 17:10), but it can also become harmful when we overstep our boundaries in rebuking others. For example, Paul asserts that he has no business to judge those who are outside of the church (1 Cor 5:12), and neither do we.

The problem is that we go to one of two extremes. We are either overly cautious and make no judgments concerning someone's sins at all. Or, we are excessively judgmental, even pronouncing judgments upon those who are outside of the church. The two most unloving and ungracious things Christians can do are to say there is no judgment and let sin go unchecked. Or, it is to stand on our soapboxes and scream about how the unsaved are going to hell. Instead, we are called to love all. That means correcting our brothers and sisters with whom we are in fellowship, but not going beyond the boundaries of the church, except in love and grace.

Are you tempted to judge those who are not Christians and condemn them to hell in your thoughts? What if your perspective shifted towards love for them? How would that change how you interact with non-Christians?

Day 89: "Ask, and it will be given to you; seek, and you will find; knock, and it will be opened to you." (7:7)

LET ME BEGIN WITH a cautionary remark: God is not a genie. Often, this verse is presented as a stand-alone solution to one's problems. If you are poor, you simply need to ask with faith, and God will give you riches. If you are ill, seek God with a trusting heart, and he will heal you. If you want a reputation, just knock, and God will open the door to opportunity. This is the false teaching of the prosperity gospel that we have already addressed. On the surface, it may look pretty and promise a lot. However, it will leave you empty and lacking in one of two ways: either falsely affirmed in faith because of worldly riches, or incorrectly condemned as faithless because you do not have the health and wealth this false "gospel" offers.

This is not what Jesus is talking about and this is not what Jesus is offering in these words here. This one verse must be read in conjunction with the next four. Otherwise, it is all too easy to abuse. We must not neglect to see that this verse is leading up to Matthew 7:11, encouraging us to ask of God who gives "good things" to his children. The problem is that we often do not know what is good for us. We might ask for wealth, only to find that we are never satisfied with how much we have. We may ask for health but lose the powerful testimony of faith amid suffering. We may ask for power and influence, and we might even gain the whole world, but we run the risk of losing our souls in the process.

Instead, we must seek the Lord and discern what the "good things" are that he desires to give us. When we learn this, we can begin to ask for things in alignment with God's will and not based on our own selfish ambitions. After all, our Father knows us so much better than we know ourselves. He knows what is good for us and what is life-giving, and he also knows what will harm us if he does give it to us. Therefore, we must be trusting in our prayers, giving ourselves over to the gracious God who desires to give what is good and who knows what is good for us.

Do you ever ask God for things you know will not be beneficial for you? What are some good things you could ask for from God? Ask for them.

Day 90: "For everyone who asks receives, and the one who seeks finds, and to the one who knocks it will be opened." (7:8)

Our God is a listener. He is not deaf or distant, but he attentively listens to every prayer we offer up to him. Now, that may not always seem to be the case, and at times it may even seem that God is intentionally not listening to us. However, the truth of the matter is that God does indeed hear every prayer we utter. Perhaps, then, the question to ask is not whether God hears, but whether we are listening in return?

We all pray and would likely affirm that God listens and responds. We are all familiar with this aspect of prayer. On the other hand, we rarely consider whether we listen when God speaks back to us, whether that be through his Word, a wise mentor, or by the Spirit. Do we give the Lord room to reply? Or, do we simply move along with our day, not giving an ear to the Lord once we have listed our requests? Unfortunately, this is often what is most lacking in many of our prayer lives. We ask and ask and ask, but never truly pause to listen for the response. Or, if we do listen for a response from God, we may ignore it if it's not the one we desired. When either of these is the case, we are not truly praying. We are ranting. We are asking God to hand over whatever we ask for, treating him like a divine ATM machine who must submit to our requests.

Instead, prayer is much more about a relationship steeped in reciprocal communication than it is about us throwing out a list of demands. We often view prayer in the latter sense, and that is perhaps why we do not feel God is listening. We have not cultivated a relationship based on communication, but one that is only based on our own talking. Don't get me wrong, it is fine to ask for things in prayer, but we fool ourselves if we think we will receive a response when we have not even learned how to listen. Instead, we must continually grow closer to the Lord whom we can approach in prayer as Father (Matt 6:9). When we do this, we will learn what the Father's heart desires for us to ask, and we will learn the sound of his voice.

Are you tempted to simply ask, but not listen? How might you culti-vate a posture of listening in your prayer life?

Day 91: "Or which one of you, if his son asks him for bread, will give him a stone?" (7:9)

JESUS COMPARES OUR PRAYER to a son asking his father for bread. Not only does this demonstrate how personal the relationship we have with God is, but it also displays the Lord's desire to give good things to his children. The hypothetical question Jesus asks resonates. Any parent in Jesus' audience would readily feel the connection that they have with their own children. Any parent, unless they are downright cruel, will do anything within their power to provide for their children. If any parent was asked by their child for something they could give that the child needs, the parent will immediately offer it up without hesitation.

Such is the relationship we have with the Lord when we come to him in prayer. But, as has been mentioned before, this does not mean God will give us anything we ask. Notice, here, the example is a piece of bread. It is basic sustenance. It is not wealth, fame, or power. It is not a perfect spouse, career, or car. It is the daily bread that Jesus mentioned back when he taught the disciples to pray (Matt 6:11). It is what we need, not necessarily what we want. Therefore, it is we who must change. It is our desires that need to shift to align with what the Lord seeks to give us. This is not to say that God does not bless some in incredible ways, and even with wealth, fame, and influence. Instead, it is to say that God is much more concerned about our daily needs than giving us things in excess.

This certainly begs the question; what about those who ask for God to provide food, yet who still go hungry? Certainly, this is the sting of this verse. However, callously throwing it around, suggesting that the needy do not ask in faith, is an abuse of God's Word. As mentioned before, the Sermon is both *here* in the present, but *not yet* fully manifest. We do see glimpses of these promises in the present, but we must also be mindful that they are *not yet* fully complete. God has not abandoned us, but he is still providentially working every moment to overthrow the sinfulness and brokenness that still plagues this life. Therefore, we pray all the more, "Come, Lord Jesus!"

Do you tend to ask God for excessive things, or things that are daily needs? If your daily needs are already met, how might you be an answer to this prayer for others?

Day 92: "Or if he asks for a fish, will give him
a serpent?" (7:10)

OUR PROBLEM IN PRAYER is that often we ask for the serpent and stone, but God gives us bread and fish instead. When we do not receive what we have asked for, we assume God is not listening or answering our prayers. We blame him for withholding the foolish things we regularly ask for. Instead, God gives us what we need rather than what we have asked for. He gives us what is beneficial, healthy, and leads to our growth, not what provides a lack of nourishment and possible harm. When this happens, we are tempted to accuse God of not providing or being an absentee father who pays us no attention.

So, we must evaluate our prayer lives in light of this. What kind of things are we praying for? Do we pray and ask God for the things that it would be cruel for him to give to us? Do we ask for things that could, in fact, destroy us if we were to have them? Even good things can do this to us. We might ask for money, and if received we may lose our hard work ethic and tenacity, ending up poorer than when we began. But perhaps, God withholds from us that which we do not need so that we may continue to rely on him. Our prayers often center around making our lives easier. However, God seems to be more interested in making us resilient and persevering.

It may be a hard path to follow, but the invitation to follow Jesus always is. This path is even difficult to follow in our prayer lives, especially when we have bread and stones confused for one another. Ask the Father for eternal life, and he will lay before you a path to the cross. Ask the Father for heavenly riches, and he will offer you a life that requires you to give freely of all you have. Ask the Father for joy and completeness, and he will require you to endure sorrow. However, if you ask of the Father, he will indeed give to you and do so freely and with more abundance than you could possibly imagine. It may cost you everything in this life, but it will mean everything in the next.

What serpents and stones do you ask for from God? What bread and fish does God give you instead?

Day 93: "If you then, who are evil, know how to give
good gifts to your children, how much more will your
Father who is in heaven give good things to those
who ask him!" (7:11)

WE CAN MOST ASSUREDLY trust our heavenly Father to give us good gifts. If we as humans, plagued by the fall and in need of redemption, can offer good things to our children, then certainly our Father who is pure, holy, and righteous will do so for us. The basis of our trust in this promise is the steadfastness of our Father's enduring character. This is the truth that the Master is pointing us towards in these verses concerning prayer. It is not to create within us false hopes about the material things we would like to have, but to create in us a persevering faith in our Father.

As mentioned before, this is often what is most lacking in our prayers. It is not that our Father does not hear or respond, but that we lack faith, or ask for things we are not intended to have. However, we do indeed have a good Father who can work through the misguided ramblings of our hearts. The Holy Spirit intercedes for us when we pray for things that may well harm us or bring us to destruction. That is how good our Father in heaven is! Not only is he there to hear the myriad requests that are lifted to him daily, but he also sends his Spirit to minister on our behalf (Rom 8:26).

Honestly, it is rather scary to imagine where we would be if the Holy Spirit were not interceding on our behalf. We would either be in a universe of despair, falsely thinking that God had abandoned us. Or, we would be living the "blessed" life, assuming we had earned everything God had given us. Either way, we would be utterly estranged from God. But our Father, in his graciousness, knows our needs and desires better than we do ourselves, and he graciously gives accordingly. For this we give him our complete trust and devotion, rooted in our knowledge of his character and his goodness. Then, along with the Holy Spirit, we ask God to reveal what is good for us, and we pray for those things.

Does your prayer life include a knowledge of how good your heavenly Father is? Do your prayers lack faithfulness?

Day 94: "So whatever you wish that others would do to you, do also to them, for this is the Law and the Prophets." (7:12)

WE OFTEN THINK OF the Law as a burdensome weight to bear. We read all the obscure laws, rituals, and requirements and wonder how it might apply to our lives today. But, here, Jesus makes it rather straightforward. Ask yourself, "How do I like to be treated? Thought of? Regarded? Approached? Loved? Cared for? Corrected?" Whatever the answers to those questions are, that is how you are to treat others. But, that's the rub of it, too. If you can answer those questions (which we all can!), then we know exactly how we are to treat others.

The problem then lies in whether we will carry it out or not. It is not a lack of knowledge, but a lack of action that prevents us from upholding Christ's command. This is, perhaps, what makes the Master's words in the Sermon so hard. They are not only theological truths to be pondered and understood, but they are truths to be lived out as well. We would prefer the former, and so often we do that with the Sermon. We think about it, teach it, study it, but we shudder at the idea of actually living it out. To avoid the demands of the Sermon, some will even suggest that Jesus is only speaking about his future kingdom. Therefore, he does not intend for the Sermon to be lived out in the present. This would be convenient if it were true. However, every bit of the Sermon demands a response and calls for its words to be obeyed. Jesus even concludes the Sermon by stating the fate of those who obey his words and those who do not (Matt 7:24-27).

Therefore, it is crucial for us to ask that original question: "How do I like to be treated?" This is where we will find the path to obedience. Jesus has already told us in the earlier parts of the Sermon how we ought to answer that question. It is to be seekers of reconciliation, givers of mercy, and lovers of our enemies. If there was any part of the Sermon that was previously vague, we need only to think of how we like to be treated. Having thought of this, we will then know what we are to do to obey the Master.

How do you like people to treat you? Who do you not treat this way?
How can you begin to treat them as you would like to be treated?

Day 95: "Enter by the narrow gate. For the gate is wide and the way is easy that leads to destruction, and those who enter by it are many." (7:13)

JESUS BEGINS THE CONCLUSION to the Sermon with these words. He has given the mandates and the stipulations for what it looks like to follow him and be his disciple, now he puts the burden on his listeners to respond. To live by what the Master teaches is the narrow gate, a path that few will choose to follow. To disregard the words of the Sermon is the path most will choose. This path is much easier to walk than the other. These paths are appropriately populated as well, with few choosing what is difficult and many choosing what is easy. One leads to life and the other, death. This is the severity with which the Sermon confronts us. It leaves no option for neutrality, nor does it offer us the convenience to delay. It summons us to respond.

This would be a wise place to check our inward motivations and desires. Are we inclined towards what is easy? Do we seek the path of least resistance or the way that is most convenient to us? Or, are we willing to go out of our way to love and serve our neighbor? Though the narrow path to follow Christ comes with many blessings, it also comes with the burdens he has laid before us in the Sermon. It comes with the burden to love, forgive, ask for forgiveness, give freely, keep our emotions in check, and uphold our promises. Furthermore, we must be certain that our motivation for doing these things is not for our own gain, but for the Lord's sake.

This is a tall order indeed, and undoubtedly a narrow path that few are willing to pursue. However, it is the path we must follow, for the alternative path leads to destruction. The early church knew this well and followed this call. One of the earliest writings we have from the church outside the Bible opens like this, "There are two ways, one of life and one of death; but a great difference between the two ways" (*Didache* 1.1). The early Apostles took to heart Christ's words, and in doing so called for the church to live out the words that Christ spoke.

Do you know if you are on the narrow or wide path? Do you choose what is easy, acceptable, and self-centered? Or, do you do what is sacrificial, loving, and costly?

Day 96: "For the gate is narrow and the way is hard that leads to life, and those who find it are few." (7:14)

WE MAY THINK THIS is too difficult a burden to bear, but we must always keep in mind the aim of the Sermon: to lead us to life. This is the purpose of the Sermon! It is given so that we might find the path to life. However, those that are on this path are few. Sadly, many of us think that we are on this path when, in reality, we are not. Rather than assume we are on the road with few, we ought to ask ourselves if we are actually on the wide and easy path with the majority of people.

This may present a sobering reality. We may find that we live with indifference to what the Sermon teaches and what it calls for our lives to look like. We must, therefore, examine our lives through the lens of the Master's words. For it is here that we can truly evaluate whether or not our actions are aligned. Naturally, we all desire to be on the path that leads to life. But, are our actions consistent with this desire? Do we only mentally assent to the teachings of the Sermon, while failing to live out what the teachings state? This is a common error we have in modern Christianity. We falsely believe that if we simply know and agree to something, it will be good enough.

However, to truly know something is to live in light of the knowledge we possess. For instance, we know that a stop sign means we need to stop before proceeding through an intersection for both our safety and the safety of others. However, if we drive through the sign without stopping, our actions declare that we do not really believe this to be the case. We have a head knowledge of what the stop sign instructs, but our actions reveal our true beliefs. Our belief is that we do not need to stop for safety. It is the same in the Sermon. We might think we know it incredibly well, perhaps have even memorized it, but this can still only be head knowledge. If we do not bring our actions into conformity with what the Master is teaching, then we do not know the Sermon at all.

Do you have only a mental knowledge of the Sermon but lack a living-knowledge of the Sermon? What parts of the Sermon do you need to begin living out?

Day 97: "Beware of false prophets, who come to you in sheep's clothing but inwardly are ravenous wolves." (7:15)

SINCE THE DAYS OF Jesus until today, there has not been a shortage of false prophets. The prophet Jeremiah had to relentlessly rebuke them in his own day (Jer 28-29). Jesus was consistently combating the false and legalistic teachings of the Pharisees and Scribes. Paul had to confront several sectarian groups in his letters. Today, the church is flooded with false doctrines and teachers who water down the gospel or manipulate it for their own ends. We have wolves in the church, brothers and sisters. Yet, they go undetected in their sheepskins, which disguise their true identity.

Jesus says these words not to scare us, but to remind us to be vigilant. We have to be wise, discerning what is true from what is false by evaluating teachings in light of what the Scriptures proclaim. Furthermore, we need to be careful. Jesus' comparison of false prophets to wolves is not without reason. Wolves are dangerous, skilled, and crafty hunters who know how to take down their prey. We must make sure that we are not their prey. We cannot only be knowledgeable of what God's Word teaches, but we also need to be able to evaluate the character, actions, and motivations of others.

As the Master warns earlier in the Sermon, there are plenty who act piously to be seen and praised (Matt 6:2, 5, 16). When the motivation of others' actions is focused on oneself and does not stem from the love of God and neighbor, we need to be wary of their teaching as well. If someone's actions are solely self-motivated, we should not be surprised that this person would be willing to consume others for their own gain. Just as a wolf has no concern for the prey it consumes, neither will false teachers care for those whom they prey upon. We have seen it too many times in recent history. "Pastors" who consume their flocks for their own financial gain, leaving the poor poorer and in spiritual distress. So how do we detect such false prophets and teachers? Fortunately, Jesus gives us some direction for detecting wolves in the verses that follow.

What false teachings have you witnessed in the church? How can we be better at detecting false teachers and helping others in the church who may be led astray?

Day 98: "You will recognize them by their fruits. Are grapes gathered from thornbushes, or figs from thistles?" (7:16)

THROUGHOUT HISTORY, THE CHURCH has suffered many false teachers. However, though they may plague the health of the Church, we are not left defenseless. We have means by which we can discern who is (and who is not) a false prophet. We simply need to evaluate their life in totality. Now, that may sound fairly straightforward, but in an individualistic and highly privatized culture, it is not so simple. It is quite easy for false prophets to hide behind the facade of their public ministry. But, when the leaves and branches are pulled back, it may reveal a thornbush hidden underneath.

This is the very type of hypocrisy that Christ is addressing in the Sermon. And, when those leaves and branches are pulled back, we learn that there was no fruit in the first place, only falsehood. So, perhaps the question to ask is, "What does the whole life of a person look like?" If we were to examine our pastors and teachers' bank accounts, would it reveal generosity or greed? If we were to examine their browsing history, would it demonstrate purity and fidelity, or a heart filled with lust? If we were to witness their interactions with their family members, would we find patience and grace, or anger and rage? It is here that we truly see what the fruit of a person is like. Even though a fake plastic tree may look good from a distance, further investigation will always reveal whether the fruit is real, or only for show.

Thus, living out the commandments of the Master requires us to be discerning, to wisely evaluate if those who teach are offering fruit or folly. There is another danger here, as well. Too often, I have witnessed poor behavior excused because of a person's talents, but this is not a valid excuse. As we will see in the next verses, what is on the inside always comes out. If we allow a thorny bramble to take root in the Church because it looks good on the outside, then we should not be surprised to find ourselves choking on the thorns later on down the road.

Are there pastors, prophets, or teachers you follow whose fruit is lacking?

Day 99: "So, every healthy tree bears good fruit, but the diseased tree bears bad fruit." (7:17)

WHAT IS ON THE inside eventually comes out. We might present ourselves as polished, successful, or having it all together. But soon enough, the fruit that is in seed form within us will blossom into the rest of our lives. As the Master will say later in Matthew's Gospel, "But what comes out of the mouth proceeds from the heart, and this defiles a person. For out of the heart come evil thoughts, murder, adultery, sexual immorality, theft, false witness, slander" (Matt 15:18-19).

Many of these same things mentioned in Matthew 15 have already been discussed in the Sermon as well. However, our temptation is to persistently conceal who we are, to leave a part of ourselves unknown to the rest of the world. We see this clearly in our use of social media. Our "lives" that are public to the world on social media convey that everything is A-Okay. We don't struggle, sin, make mistakes, or go through difficulties in the online versions of our lives. No, in the world of social media, we have already achieved the "perfect" versions of ourselves that we are striving for. However, we only have to take one honest look at ourselves in the mirror to come to the realization that we often present a falsified version of who we are. We may try to lie to the outside world about who we are and the type of fruit we produce but, if we are honest with ourselves, we know our external fruit does not always match who we really are on the inside.

Furthermore, the fruit within us cannot stay hidden. It comes out, and it does so because it is nestled in the very center of who we are. Therefore, the part of ourselves which should receive the most attention and growth is within us, not outside. Rather than focusing on producing fruit that looks good externally, we must stare into the deep recesses of our own hearts and find the idols lurking there. When we look there, we will find no shortage of rotten fruit waiting to come out. It may not be visible to the world around us at the moment, but if it is at the core of who we are, then it most certainly will become manifest. So, we must honestly look inward and address the sin lurking there that we keep hidden from the rest of the world.

What type of fruit is within you? What would it look like if it were to come out? How long might it be until it does?

Day 100: "A healthy tree cannot bear bad fruit,
nor can a diseased tree bear good fruit." (7:18)

IN CONTRAST TO THE fruit of diseased trees, there is also the fruit of healthy trees. Again, the fruit that is within is what eventually comes out. If there is love, peace, and mercy within our hearts, it is certain to move outwardly into the rest of our lives. It cannot help but take root and grow, expressing itself in how we relate to others and interact with the world around us. Often, however, we are a combination of the two trees the Master tells us about. Our lives are a mixture, neither entirely good nor bad, but a blend of both healthy and diseased fruit, and both types of fruit routinely come out in our lives.

The goal then is to learn how to plant and cultivate healthy fruit. There is plenty of diseased fruit within us, so we must begin to uproot it and replant it with good seeds that will grow into healthy trees. Now, how do we go about such a thing? The answer is what we have been looking at all along! It is to embrace Jesus' words in the Sermon. It is to live the life that is found in the beatitudes. It is to turn the other cheek, to be reconciled with our brothers and sisters, to be gracious and forgiving while also confessing our own sin. Jesus calls us to a life that is uniform throughout, consistent inside and outside, with no degrees of separation in who we are privately and publicly.

It is these seeds that we must begin to grow in our hearts. I know for myself that can be a rather terrifying notion. My own life is often out of sync, and I daily recognize how much diseased fruit is lurking below and sprouting up to the surface. The daily call to follow Jesus is truly a fight and a struggle, one in which we must routinely die to ourselves. However, it is on this soil, the soil that is tilled when we die to ourselves, that we can plant the seeds that will bring forth healthy fruit that will bless ourselves and the world around us.

What trees need to be uprooted in your life? What trees need to be planted there instead? What trees in your life need to stay rooted, and how do you cultivate them to their fullest potential?

Day 101: "Every tree that does not bear good fruit
is cut down and thrown into the fire." (7:19)

WE CANNOT FORGET THAT these past verses are addressing how to recognize false prophets. These verses, however, do have applications for us as well. We must heed the words of the Master who challenges us throughout the Sermon to be consistent in all that we are, internally and externally. These verses tell us that those who do not produce good fruit are judged for their false deeds. Although the words here are primarily focused on false teachers, we cannot forget that Jesus will expand this teaching to all people in the final judgment (Matt 25:31-46).

Therefore, we must embrace a lifestyle that conforms to the teachings of the Master as well. We must take seriously Christ's teaching that those who do not produce good fruit will enter judgment. This is certainly not an easy teaching, but it is nevertheless true. And, since it is true, we must consider the full scope of its meaning regarding our own lives. We must seriously ask whether or not our own lives are producing good, healthy, and useful fruit? We must also seriously ask whether those who are prophets and teachers live in such a way that is consistent with the teachings of the Master. The fruit of our lives is the indicator for what is on the inside and, just as James writes, "So also faith by itself, if it does not have works, is dead" (Jas 2:17).

Our fruit must match our faith, but we often separate the two. We relegate faith to a place where it only pertains to our thoughts and what we think, forgetting that our beliefs (our faith) are meant to be active. The truth is that our fruit stems from our beliefs, and we are always acting according to what we believe. If we really believe that Jesus is who he says he says, then we will act in accordance with what he commands. If we believe Jesus truly is the Son of God, then the fruit of our lives will reflect our beliefs through obedience. We will follow the Master who calls us not to be prideful and pompous, lying and lustful, or angry and arrogant. Instead, the Master calls us to be lowly and loving, prayerful and peaceful, fasting and forgiving.

What does your fruit look like? What does it say about what you truly believe? Do your faith and works complement one another?

Day 102: "Thus you will recognize them
by their fruits." (7:20)

THE OLD ADAGE, "ACTIONS speak louder than words," seems to apply here. Are you trying to discern whether someone (or yourself) is a false prophet or teacher? Simply look at the type of fruit that is produced in their lives. Does the way a person acts match what they say, or is there a dissonance between the two? Of course, our actions are not the summation of who we are as people, but they still have much to say about us. It is by our fruit, our actions, that people recognize who we really are.

Think of it like this: In a marriage, imagine one spouse who only said, "I love you," but never demonstrated that love. After some time, the other spouse would begin to question whether these words are actually meant. The statement alone, divorced from the fruit of actions, becomes meaningless. There is no way to verify its truth. So it is with our obedience to Christ. We can claim to follow Christ but still be entirely lacking in fruit. When this is the case, we have to ask ourselves if what we say we believe and confess is really what we believe. If only our actions were evaluated (not what we say), would there be enough evidence to convict us of actually having faith? Or, would the fruit of our lives reveal that we don't really believe all that we proclaim?

This, my friends, is where the Sermon smacks us in the face with a wake-up call. When we ask if our actions convey the faith we proclaim, we can better see our shortcomings. This is not to suggest that our actions are what earn our salvation. That would be legalism, and it is a misconstrual of the gospel of grace. But God's grace, which produces faith within us, will spill over into the rest of our lives and produce good and healthy fruit. Faith cannot merely be mental agreement and nothing more, for that would diminish God's grace which transforms every aspect of who we are. The gospel of grace, instead, remakes our whole being and entire lives. Anything less and we have settled for an insufficient gospel which does not save.

You are recognized by your fruit. So, what are others going to recognize about you?

Day 103: "Not everyone who says to me, 'Lord, Lord,' will enter the kingdom of heaven, but the one who does the will of my Father who is in heaven." (7:21)

PUT BLUNTLY, LIP SERVICE counts for very little when it comes to the Kingdom of Heaven. We can pray as loudly as possible and use as many words as we want, or sing at the top of our lungs and confess to the gospel a million times over, and it still won't be enough. That is because the words of our mouths count for very little compared to our actions, as it is our actions that reveal what we truly believe. Notice, it is those who *do* the will of the Father who enter the Kingdom of Heaven. The Christian faith is one of action, not one in which we simply say or think the right things.

In light of this, we must leave behind any notion that we can talk our way into the kingdom. Our "Christianese" may sound impressive and fool those around us, but the Master sees through this idle talk and hollow words. And note, it is not that the words we speak and things we may say are altogether wrong. They may even be truthful on every level. However, when these words are not backed up by the rest of our lives, they become nothing more than meaningless sounds escaping our mouths. Anyone can cry out "Lord, Lord," but to live in dependence and obedience on God's name is something else entirely.

Now, Paul does say, "For everyone who calls on the name of the Lord will be saved" (Rom 10:13). But Paul, quoting the prophet Joel (Joel 2:32), is not talking about saying some magic words to be saved. No! Paul is talking about the name of the Lord, which means staking everything we know and trust in the character and person of God. Calling on the name of the Lord is not soothsaying for salvation, but it is a conviction and mindset that stirs us within. It is taking God seriously for who he is, claiming and confessing to his holy and perfect nature and trusting that the Lord who is merciful will come to the rescue. This, my friends, is much different than casually throwing around the holy name of the Lord and assuming that we have covered all the bases. Calling on the name of the Lord is trusting in the Lord and his character, as well as taking seriously the Lord's commands and living in obedience to him.

In what ways do you cry out, "Lord, Lord!"? Is it only lip service, or do you confess that Jesus is Lord with your life as well?

Day 104: "On that day many will say to me, 'Lord, Lord, did we not prophesy in your name, and cast out demons in your name, and do many mighty works in your name?'" (7:22)

WE MIGHT THINK THAT Jesus is contradicting much of the Sermon here. As we just saw, it is indeed our actions that matter and not just our speech. But, what about the mighty works mentioned in this verse? Wouldn't such acts of faith be the good deeds that corroborate an inward life of faith? Wouldn't these actions be the walk that backs up the talk? Well, perhaps. . . But, again, they may simply be further examples of the hypocritical acts mentioned in chapter 6 of the Sermon. They may simply be done for show and for earthly praise.

It is also important to note that these works, which are not inherently wrong in and of themselves, are typically associated with what it means to be a religious and devout person. Yet even these acts are not enough for entry to the Kingdom of Heaven. Furthermore, in the Sermon, Jesus nowhere calls for us to perform such deeds or states that this is what it means to follow him and be his disciple.

This again reminds us that our inward being, the place from which these acts spring, is what truly matters. Not only are these acts insufficient, but they are easily abused and misused so that the glory may point toward us rather than our Father in heaven. Instead, Jesus has already given us a list of deeds in the Sermon to perform: don't be angry, lustful, quick to divorce, rash in our speech, retaliatory, or hateful. But instead, be forgiving and giving, love your enemies, and do these things through prayer and fasting. What the Master calls us to in the Sermon is much more ordinary than prophesying, casting out demons, and doing mighty works.

It is mundane wonders we are called to perform, not mighty works. What we are called to in the Sermon is achievable in everyday life. It doesn't require a special anointing of the Holy Spirit or some profound gifting from the Lord. Instead, it requires compassion, honesty, humility, and mercy, just as we witness in the life of the Master. The actions that flow from someone who is seeking the kingdom are these mundane wonders, not the "mighty works" that will bring us fame and honor while robbing glory from the Lord. My friends, it is not the "mighty works" we must strive for, but mundane wonders!

Which kind of actions do you admire most, the "mighty works" or the mundane wonders?

Day 105: "And then will I declare to them,
'I never knew you; depart from me, you workers
of lawlessness.'" (7:23)

THE KEY WORD IN this verse is *never*. It is not as though Jesus knew these "workers of lawlessness" at a different time or stage of life. Nor is it that Jesus somewhat knew them, but did not really know them too well. It is that Jesus *never* knew these people. And these people are the ones crying out, "Lord, Lord!" in the previous verse. Outward piety and mighty works do not make us known by Christ. Instead, Christ knows those who follow his commands. Namely, the commands that he has listed throughout the Sermon. It is these acts that garner his attention and are a true fulfillment of the law.

Once again, let us be reminded that Jesus is not against the law. Here, he even calls those who fail to obediently follow the Sermon "workers of lawlessness." It is not that we have scrapped the law and done away with it. It is that we fail to live out what is most important in the law: loving God with all our heart, mind, and soul and loving our neighbor as ourselves (Matt 22:36-40). This is the law that Christ desires for us to live out. This is the law that brings us into a relationship with the Lord in which we are known by him. This is the law that the Sermon on the Mount has been pointing us towards all along. It is about appropriately ordering what we love so that our love is no longer inwardly focused and selfish, but outward reaching, focused on God and others.

This does not mean we do not love and care for ourselves, but it means that we also love and care for others in the same way we do for ourselves. That means forgiving others as we would like to be forgiven. Giving generously, as we hope others would do when we are in need. It means not pointing out shortcomings in others when we know there is a log in our own eyes that could be pointed out. It is this person, the one who does these things, who is known by the Master. It is those who pray, give, and fast out of their love and devotion to the Lord, rather than for the praise of others, who uphold the law according to Christ. And, my friend, when we do such things, we are lovingly known by our Father in heaven.

Does Jesus know you? What parts of your life might make Jesus know you a little better?

Day 106: "Everyone then who hears these words of mine and does them will be like a wise man who built his house on the rock." (7:24)

THIS IS THE CALL to the life of the kingdom. It is a call to obedience, as well as a warning. It is a summons to respond to the Sermon and for us to determine whether we will follow the teaching that Jesus has just given, or will we refuse it? If we are obedient, then we are building something strong and steadfast. We are building a house with a firm foundation. We are building a life that stands upon solid ground that will not be shaken. The words of the Master call for us to be steady in an uncertain world. However, the certainty of this life is not found in jobs, money, and so forth. Our steadfastness in life is founded upon obedience to Christ's words, which teach us how we are to properly love God and neighbor.

This is an invitation to a completely different way of being in the world, to live by a different set of values. While the kingdoms of the world beckon us towards power, position, and prestige, the call to Christ's kingdom runs contrary. Instead, it encourages us to become weak for the sake of others, to sacrifice on their behalf, and to value others as we value ourselves. It is here that we find our sure footing in life. By placing our allegiance in Christ and living out the laws of citizenship for his kingdom, we are well-grounded and stand firmly on the rock of God's living Word.

The book of James echoes Christ's words, affirming that we cannot merely hear the Sermon and not obey. "But be doers of the word, and not hearers only, deceiving yourselves" (Jas 1:22). If we only hear or read the Sermon, but fail to implement it into our lives, we are fooling ourselves. If so, we are just like the hypocrites who are mentioned throughout the Sermon who think they can justify themselves by their "pious" deeds, but who fail to love God and neighbor. But we cannot fool God. He knows us, and he knows us quite well. He knows whether we are obedient and living out what Christ has called us to do, or whether we have allowed the words of Christ to simply pass through our ears but not into our hearts.

What is your foundation in life? What are you building the house that is your life upon?

Day 107: "And the rain fell, and the floods came, and the winds blew and beat on that house, but it did not fall, because it had been founded on the rock." (7:25)

JUST BECAUSE WE OBEY the words of the Master does not mean we will not face trouble in this world. Though our lives are indeed much better when we heed the words of Christ, this is not to suggest that every problem we come across will vanish due to our obedience to Christ. This is the false doctrine that the prosperity gospel teaches. However, nearly every page of the Bible speaks against it. Instead, this verse reminds us that even though troubles will come, we will be able to weather the storm because we have built our lives on the foundation of God's Word. Calamity and destruction will come, but we can stand against these forces as we are held securely in Christ. We are held fast by Christ who keeps us grounded when the winds and storms of life would blow us to and fro.

Therefore, when such circumstances arise, we must not look at the conditions that assail us. We will see in two verses that the same woes come to those who disobey Christ's teaching as well. Instead, we look to our foundation and ask ourselves, "What sort of foundation am I building? Do I build my foundation on the shifting sands that this world calls secure? Or, do I build my life upon the foundation of the Lord and his Word, which cannot be shaken?" Asking such questions is imperative in the life of following Christ. These questions serve as diagnostics that help us determine what sort of building plans we are using for constructing our lives. I know for myself, when I ask such questions, I quite often determine that my life is built upon the temporary securities of this world.

Friend, if that is you right now, there is still hope. In such situations, we simply need to pause, hit reset, and go back to the basics. We start, once again, at the beginning of the Sermon and do so considering how we might build the foundations of Christ's kingdom into our lives. We begin asking, as the beatitudes do, am I poor in spirit? Mournful? Meek? Do I hunger and thirst for righteousness or the riches of the world? When we seek the answers to these questions, we begin anew to build our lives upon Christ's sure and firm foundation.

Which kingdom are you building your life upon? Do you obey Jesus' teaching in the Sermon or not? What does this tell you about the kingdom you are founding your life upon?

Day 108: "And everyone who hears these words of mine and does not do them will be like a foolish man who built his house on the sand." (7:26)

UNFORTUNATELY, A MAJORITY OF those who hear the Master's teachings will be like the foolish man, choosing not to obey the words of Christ. A majority will choose to build their lives upon the sinking sands of this world, which offer no stability. Jesus has already warned that those who enter and walk by the wide and easy path will be led to destruction (Matt 7:13). Here, we are reminded again that many will choose this path by disobeying Christ.

To hear and not obey is our great temptation as well. We might hear these words and agree with them, but then fool ourselves into thinking we obey just because we agree. However, this is not what Christ tells us. He instead tells us that we must live out the words of the Sermon in our lives. If we only agree with Christ's teaching but never let it manifest in our lives, then we have built our lives upon sand just the same as someone who would outright reject Christ's teaching. My friends, agreement is our adversary when it comes to obeying Christ. Agreement will dilute our thinking and never cause us to evaluate our actions. We must instead have a steadfast devotion and obedience in our pursuit to follow Christ. We must take an honest look to see whether we have moved past cheap and easy agreement to costly and difficult obedience. The former is a foundation of sand that will only uphold for a short time but will ultimately come crashing down when adversity comes. The latter, costly and difficult obedience, secures us on a firm foundation that will prevail when troubles come.

So, my brothers and sisters, what foundation are you going to choose? Remember, the firm foundation requires action, whereas the weak foundation is easily found through cheap agreement. We must not be deceived into thinking that hearing Christ's words comes at no cost. No, my friends, the words of Christ cost and demand everything from us. They require our entire lives, and nothing less will do. But, when we surrender our lives, we gain the life of Christ that is eternal, unfading, and imperishable.

Have you fallen for the lie that agreement with Christ's words is enough? If so, what more is Christ asking of you in your life?

Day 109: "And the rain fell, and the floods came, and the winds blew and beat against that house, and it fell, and great was the fall of it." (7:27)

YOU WILL NOTICE THAT the circumstances that fall on those who are obedient and disobedient to Christ's words are the same. Guaranteed for all is adversity and strife, disappointment and despair, trouble and travail. Whether we obey Christ or not, nothing offers us immunity from living in a sinful and broken world. We are all susceptible to the ills that life brings our way, and we will all experience various degrees of suffering.

So, the question is not whether trouble will come or not, but to determine if our lives are built upon a foundation that can withstand it. If we forsake the teachings of the Master, the troubles of this world will bring our lives crashing down. We will be blown against and beaten down, and we will have no sure foundation to secure us during these moments. Furthermore, we cannot limit what Jesus is speaking about here to only this life. It is crucial to recall that Jesus said just a few verses earlier, "Not everyone who says to me, 'Lord, Lord,' will enter the kingdom of heaven. . ." (Matt 7:21). Jesus is speaking beyond everyday life and the troubles of this world. He is also talking about the coming Kingdom of Heaven, and it is for this moment that we must spend our lives in preparation. At this moment, Jesus will judge the earth, and his judgment will come like a storm, exposing the foundations of our lives and revealing what lies beneath the surface.

This may sound rather terrifying and daunting, and it no doubt is. But we must remember that building a secure foundation is obeying Christ's words. That is difficult at times, and we are prone to failure, but if we strive to bring the Sermon into every part of our lives, we build a stronger foundation each day. This is not to say that actions grant us entry to Christ's kingdom. But if we truly follow Christ, then our actions will reflect this. Jesus is the one sure foundation upon which we build our lives. If we love him, believe in him, trust him, fear him, long to be with him, then we must certainly be obedient to him as well.

What is your foundation? Is it Christ? Is it able to withstand the day of judgment? Or, is it time to make Christ your foundation?

Day 110: "And when Jesus finished these sayings, the crowds were astonished at his teaching . . . " (7:28)

YOU MAY RECALL THAT when Jesus began the Sermon, he purposefully withdrew from the crowds, intending to speak only to his disciples (Matt 5:1). Now, a larger audience has gathered around the Master as he has laid out the principles of the kingdom. They are eager to hear these revolutionary words that Christ is speaking. And not only were the crowds eager to hear the Lord's message, but they were also astonished by the teaching itself.

Relating this to ourselves, we might ask how we respond to Christ's message. Are we so interested in his Word that we'll go out of our way to hear it? Are we willing to leave our routine day behind to go up the mountain and sit at the Master's feet? If so, do his words still strike us with amazement, or have they become rote and dull? These are pertinent questions to ask, and perhaps it is time we reevaluate how we receive God's Word. Of course, we cannot force ourselves to be astonished if we have known God's Word for a long time. But that does not mean we forsake our discipline to carefully and regularly study Scripture. We must renew our devotion, our dedication, our obedience, and our trust. We must renew our commitment to being shaped and formed daily by Scripture. To do so, we will have to realign some of our priorities.

Let's be honest, pausing in our day to read the Bible is not pragmatic by worldly standards. But, my friends, we do not belong to this world. If we are in Christ, we are citizens of another kingdom, and we must prepare ourselves for it by learning the law of love that governs that land. We must learn how we will live in that kingdom so we can begin to practice it in our lives today. In doing so, we invite the eternal into the everyday. We become a part of Christ's prayer from this very sermon, "Your kingdom come, your will be done, on earth as it is in heaven" (Matt 6:10). So, brothers and sisters, let us press onward in the calling that Christ has placed on our lives, advancing towards the kingdom with self-abandon, forsaking this world for Christ and his kingdom.

Do Christ's words still affect you the same way they have before? How might you renew your commitment to God's Word? What needs to shift to make it a priority?

Day 111: ". . .for he was teaching them as one who had authority, and not as their scribes." (7:29)

THERE IS SOMETHING UNIQUE about Christ's words. Something palpable that causes those who hear them to respond and be moved by them. Deep within us, we know that what Christ instructs is how we ought to behave. Yet, in life, our desires wage war against what the Sermon commands. Oddly, on the surface, the words of the Sermon are nothing extraordinary. They are not some brand new way of thinking or a breakthrough discovery on interpersonal relationships with God and neighbor. In fact, they are quite simple and could be boiled down to loving God and our neighbors. In their truest sense, they are what it is to be a good human being.

However, when Christ speaks these words, there is something else at work. That is because these words are not just from any other person, but they are coming from God himself. Thus, they carry a weight and significance that other human speech does not. They are qualitatively different from the words we utter daily. This is because the source is unique, and so is the authority that the source bears. Even if I were to recite the Sermon word for word, it is still entirely unlike when Christ speaks it. When I say the words of the Sermon, I speak them as a hypocrite. I commend the words of the Sermon, while also being a violator of the very words I speak. This is the case for all of us. Each of us fails in some regard to uphold the Sermon.

In contrast, Christ speaks the words of the Sermon as the perfect fulfillment of these words. He has lived out every word of the Sermon in perfect obedience and, therefore, holds the authority to command others to do the same. As both the Son of God and the true and perfect embodiment of the words of the Sermon, Christ speaks with an unquestioned authority that rings clear through history to us today. So here, at the end of the Sermon, there is only one thing left to ask. Will we receive Christ's words as authoritative over every aspect of our lives, or not? Will we choose to obey the one who holds all authority over heaven and earth, or will we choose our own false notions of authority? That is the choice before us. So, what will we choose?

Whose authority do you live under? Yours, or Christ's? How will you respond to the Sermon?

Conclusion

THERE IS NO DOUBT that the Sermon on the Mount is challenging. When we hear the words Christ speaks, we are struck with a powerful message that challenges us to the very core of our beings. We are confronted on every issue. Every idol we once held dear must be laid down at the feet of the Master as we surrender the counterfeit gods in our lives for the one true King. This is no easy task, as the idols we have invited into our lives have become routine, rote, and even cherished. We unconsciously worship them, completely unaware of the hold they have on our lives. This is where the Sermon is of immense value. It forces us to look at our lives with the utmost scrutiny. In doing so, we often quickly find the idols that have taken root in our hearts. They are painful to remove, but they must be uprooted.

My friend, as you have read through these pages, my hope is that you are not only challenged but encouraged as well. Though we cannot live up to everything the Sermon requires, we worship a God who sent his Son to do so on our behalf and lived out the Sermon's commands to perfection. For this, we are to be exceedingly grateful, knowing that God does not look for perfect obedience and unwavering faith in us, but in Christ. Christ has been perfectly obedient and unwaveringly faithful on our behalf. However, we cannot let this lead to apathy on our part. Instead, we should love Christ all the more and seek to follow him more closely each day. Seeing how Christ has demonstrated the law of love and grace in his life, so too should we seek to embrace this law with every fiber of our being.

I hope that as you read these words you found areas of your life that need to be reconciled to Christ. I hope you have confronted misplaced desires, selfish ambitions, and false idols that need to be surrendered to God. I know that I do with every encounter with the Sermon. There have been moments in writing this where I have had to pause and repent of my ways. On more than one occasion, I have once more heard myself mutter, "Ouch," underneath my breath in response to the Sermon. Christ has again cut through to my soul and begun to pry an idol out of my heart. The Sermon confronts all of us in powerful ways. So, may we all continue to surrender our hearts and desires to God. And may we do so with a renewed hope, knowing that our Lord is gracious and merciful, abounding in steadfast love, and quick to forgive. That is our hope, a God who loves us so dearly that he will go any length necessary to offer us forgiveness. That forgiveness is found in the Master. May we daily bow down at his feet.

May the grace and peace of Christ be upon you. Amen.

Made in the USA
Columbia, SC
28 November 2022

72188537R00070